Aerphobics

The Scientific Way To Stop Exercising

Don Lessem

William Morrow and Company, Inc.
New York ——————————— 1980

Book design by Frank J. Cangelosi

Library of Congress Cataloging in Publication Data

Lessem, Don.
  Aerphobics.

  Includes index.
  1. Exercise—Anecdotes, facetiae, satire,
etc. I. Title.
PN6231.E9L4   818'.5407   80-12212
ISBN 0-688-03663-5
ISBN 0-688-08663-2 (pbk.)

Printed in the United States of America

First Edition
1 2 3 4 5 6 7 8 9 10

To my father
LAWRENCE LESSEM
Who looks good in everything he eats

With compelling and irrefutable logic, Don Lessem observes in *Aerphobics*, "Becoming fit is an arduous task and a never-ending one, for one can always be more fit. Whereas physical fitness may once have been essential to our daily living, it is now so irrelevant that those who wish to attain it must exercise in their leisure hours." Carrying this logic to its conclusion, the science of aerphobics asks, Why bother?

Relying on the program established by the Sedentary Institute of Technology (SIT), *Aerphobics* explains how to snap the obsession with health and fitness and learn how best to be out of shape. Beginning with the Seven-Day De-Oxification Program, *Aerphobics* proceeds through a variety of techniques to help the exercise addict kick his habit and achieve that state of nirvana that lies just the other side of sloth and catatonia.

Acknowledgments

PHOTOGRAPHS BY TED DILLARD
ILLUSTRATIONS BY MARTHA DILLARD

Thanks for being good-humored photographic subjects go to:
Don Ashe, Ken Ashe, Tom Bergendahl, Chris Bongiardina,
Amy Brown, Drew Brown, Mary Davis, Matthew Furtney,
Paula Hartstein, Bobby Hazel, David Hazel, Nancy Hazel,
Lori Keiran, Eric Kraus, Wendy Kraus, Bob Fontaine, Julia
Mears, Clark Swain, and Debi Zimmerman. And thanks to
Bob Bender, my editor, for sharing the aerphobic perspec-
tive. All remaining, unaccounted-for thanks go to The Twink.

Contents

Introduction

Your cheeks are hollow, your limbs gaunt. You are often thirsty, rarely hungry. A feeling of restlessness frequently overcomes you. You disappear from company suddenly, and return with eyes brightened, skin glistening, and breathing labored. Your speech is disjointed, filled with odd, unfamiliar phrases such as, "did forty laps before I cramped," "bent the *dérailleur* when I slipped on the toe clips," or "got a stitch doing fartlek."

Do you recognize these symptoms? Does this sound like you, or one near and dear to you?

These are the warning signs of an epidemic disease, a contagion that has struck 100 million Americans. The symptoms are much the same as those of amphetamine freaks, Whirling Dervishes, or Stillman water-dieters. But by sheer weight of numbers, this is a dependency many times more powerful than drugs, religion, or self-improvement.

The disease is exercise. Masquerading cleverly as a cure, it is infecting millions more each year, preying on the young and old alike. Exercise threatens to destroy our familiar physiques, our common pleasures, our family life, our economy; in short, the entire fabric of modern life.

Can it be stopped? Yes, there is hope. The very fact that you are reading this book, presumably sitting down, or at least standing still, indicates that the tide can yet be stemmed. It is our fervent hope that this book will provide you with the ammunition to fight exercise, by analyzing its spurious benefits and dubious origins from a physiological, sociological, and psychological perspective. What more can you ask in a cheap paperback?

But this is not all that *Aerphobics* provides. It gives you the proven strategies with which you can rid yourself, once and for all, of the exercise monkey on your back. A gamut of treatments is offered to deal with every form of activity addiction and every misguided motivation.

Were this book to deal only with causation and treatment, it would be simply *the* definitive work on the exercise syndrome, a likely best seller, and a possible Pulitzer Prize candidate.

Yet *Aerphobics* also presents an explication, a holistic rationalization, as it were, for why we are the way we are: fat, lazy, and sluggish. *Aerphobics* is a way of life, *our* way of life, the route to happiness, health, and painless—though regrettably early—death. Through this miraculous book, you will learn not only how to arrest the exercise-related decline of your life, but also how to reorient yourself on the path to unimagined fulfillment. Believe me, I should know. I'm a doctor.

DR. MELVIN PRACTISS, D.D.S.

Mardi Gras, 1980
Villa Hefti, Brazil

PART I

Aerphobics and You

What Is Aerphobics?

Aerphobics, in simplest terms, is the avoidance of exercise. True as that statement is, it is as much an oversimplification as saying Einstein's Theory of Relativity has something to do with *Star Wars*. Aerphobics is a science, a philosophy, a logical basis for all the quit-exercising programs outlined in this guide.

The modern plague of joggers, cyclists, swimmers, and skiers is in large part the result of the work of one man, Dr. Kenneth Cooper. Cooper is the author of a best-selling series of books on a fitness regimen he calls "Aerobics." Cooper found that circulatory conditioning could be improved by regular, steady endurance exercise. According to current theory, such exercise must be performed four times per week for longer than five minutes at a pulse rate exceeding 150 beats per minute.

Aerobic "sports" are those that require such continuous motion, and so exclude the true competitive sports that test strategy and skill, as well as fitness. So bocci, shuffleboard, Go Fish, Parcheesi, and other favorite pastimes are excluded from the fitness programs of many aerobics practitioners.

Many strenuous exercises involve "anaerobic" stress, to toss in another confusing phrase. When running fast or lifting a heavy weight, the struggling body calls upon its own energy reserves rather than drawing on oxygen, or aerobic respiration. So even the best-conditioned sprinter cannot go more than a minute before falling over, and you and I get out of breath after lifting a fork.

So millions have now taken up jogging, bicycling, rope-skipping, swimming, and cross-country skiing as preferred forms of aerobic conditioning; activities which leave them friendless, boring, self-absorbed, and exhausted.

Dr. Cooper himself designed a twelve-minute test of aerobic fitness, requiring the participant to run as far as possible, without undue strain, in that period of time. Nevertheless, some competitive types actually succeeded in killing themselves with the test, which apparently indicated that they were not in the best of physical condition. Such unfortunate occurrences, rare as they are, do point up two of the major problems of the aerobic fitness program: we are not in shape and we cannot be relied upon to get ourselves in shape.

Exercise, whether aerobic or anaerobic[1] is tiring. Exercise devotees say that we must tire ourselves in order to be less tired—a leap of faith that makes the Olympic long jump look like hopscotch.

ACTIVITY ENDURANCE LIMIT

Exercise Type		
ANAEROBIC	SPRINTING	25 seconds
	WEIGHT LIFTING	3 minutes[2]
	SPEED SKATING	20 minutes
	SLALOM SKIING	33 minutes
	BASKETBALL	2 hours 45 minutes

1. Or claustrophobic, in the case of squash.
2. Somewhat longer for weight dropping.

AEROBIC	TENNIS	4 hours 15 minutes
	BASEBALL	8 hours [3]
	GOLF	9 hours 34 minutes
	PINOCHLE	12 hours 23 minutes [4]
AERPHOBIC	WIENIE ROASTING	15 hours
	WINE TASTING	18 hours
	SNORING	40 years [5]

On the other hand, the science of aerphobics carries this reasoning to its logical crux—why bother? Becoming fit is an arduous task and a never-ending one, for one can always be more fit. Whereas physical fitness may once have been essential to our daily living, it is now so irrelevant that those who wish to attain it must exercise in their leisure hours. And fitness itself counts for little against the threats of a modern world; your pulse rate before impact is of little import when you kiss a truck at highway speeds.

Becoming fit is clearly not enjoyable, or why would so many of us be so unfit? Aerphobics encourages us to do what we do best: sit, eat, and sleep. Though the term itself may be unfamiliar, the aerphobic life is the one embraced by the vast majority of citizens. It is the sedentary, consuming Life of Riley to which we are long accustomed. Exercise of any sort is a disruption, emotionally and physically, to that way of life, a needless and possibly dangerous shock.

Mental health is of course related to physical well-being. The aerobics craze has led many of us to question our own health and life-style. Aerphobics gives those insecure ones amongst us the pseudo-scientific jargon to justify the activities we do daily. We can go on, happier in the knowledge that we have nothing to feel guilty about. The full weight of economics, history, literature, religion, and psychology is behind the aerphobics movement as we shall see, and so we

3. Playing endurance here far exceeds viewer patience (see Met effect).
4. Longer without kibbitzing.
5. See R. Van Winkle on effects of bowling.

Effect of traffic accident on aerobe

Effect of traffic accident on aerphobe

must not just grudgingly accept ourselves, but instead, embrace our life-style and ourselves—at least as far as our stubby little arms can reach.

So rip open a six-pack, grab a Ring-Ding, lie down on the couch, and turn on the game. Relax, doze off, content in the knowledge that you are living aerphobically.

LEVELS OF AEROBIC EXERCISE AND THEIR CONSEQUENCES

"Sport"	Beginner	Novice	Expert	Fanatic
BICYCLING	4 miles damp crotch	16 miles sore crotch	64 miles no crotch	256 miles crutch
SWIMMING	¼ mile water in ear	1 mile water in nose	4 miles water in lungs	16 miles drowning
JUMPING ROPE	15 minutes headaches	1 hour sore arches	4 hours flattened arches	16 miles flattened head (see neighbor)
X-COUNTRY SKIING	½ mile runny nose	2 miles windburn	4 miles freezer burn	16 miles Farewell to Arms
DANCING	1 hour broken shoe	4 hours broken out	16 hours broken foot	64 hours bad vibes
RUNNING	1 mile breathlessness	4 miles mindlessness	16 miles aimlessness	64 miles lifelessness

A Talk with the Founder of Aerphobics

In the course of preparing this tome we had the rare opportunity to interview the father of the Aerphobics Way, Dr. Mel Practiss, while he was in Malibu, California, to dedicate the new Maynard G. Krebs Idleness Center. What follows is a transcript of our conversation with "Papa Doc" in its entirety:

Q. How did the aerphobic movement come about?
A. We prefer not to use the term "movement," as it connotes motion. Aerphobics actually has been around since civilization began, possibly longer. It's nothing more than the enjoyment of life. The Greeks called it hedonism, to the French it is *"joie de vivre,"* to Eddie Cantor it was "whoopee."

Q. But how did it acquire the name "aerphobics"?
A. Of late, too many people were questioning the modern way of life, exercise being the most insidious form of this pervasive nihilism. While most of us had not changed, we'd begun to doubt the health, wisdom, and propriety of laziness, so I felt a catchy phrase and a little scientific dressing might rekindle the faith. It's much the way "TM" and "alpha waves" brought back daydreaming. Also, my lawyer advised me to patent a name for tax reasons.

Q. Was it your medical background which convinced you of the value of aerphobics?

A. Yes, I do feel that dentistry gave me the solid technical training to pursue the physiological approach to nonexercise. For years, I saw each day how much more comfortable my patients were sitting down than I was standing up, that is, until I started working on them. It was then that I began formulating the concept of the aerphobic life-style.

Q. And where did it go from there?

A. I first detailed my philosophy to one of my patients, Mr. Ralph Sobel, while giving him a root canal. He was fascinated. I remember him staring at me, speechless, tears coming to his eyes.

Q. He was impressed?

A. Yes. He thought the idea had great sales potential. Mr. Sobel was a press agent at the time. Together we formed the Sedentary Institute of Technology and began marketing the aerphobics package.

Q. But it was my understanding that extensive research and planning went into the development of the aerphobics system.

A. I know. The Better Business Bureau has been after us without success for many years.

Q. No, I was referring to scientific research.

A. Indeed. Well, after Mr. Sobel left the corporation to pursue other interests, I became more actively involved in research to substantiate the claims I'd made in my first book, *How to Be Your Own Couch* ($3.95, Harcourt Brace Sonovavitch). The FAT CITY clinics were opened and I began to personally treat the terminally active.

Q. You've been expanding in other directions, haven't you?

A. If you're referring to my weight, I don't appreciate that remark. We are now heavily into aerphobics-related industries. I've got three imitation-marshmallow factories, a chain of drive-in coronary care units, and I've just inked an international agreement with Giancana-Bonano, Inc., of Palermo to produce all our specialty items.

Q. What has made you so concerned with the plight of the athlete?

A. I've said earlier that I see this exercise craze as a potential threat to the predominance of the aerphobic life-style. That's why I founded Aerobics Anonymous, that's why I evolved the many techniques which you've been commissioned to outline in this book.

Q. About that commission. I still haven't received a contract.

A. Odd you should mention that. I've just put one out on you.

Q. I see. Thank you for your time then, sir. I must be going.

A. Did my secretary mention my interview fee?

The Sedentary Institute of Technology

Where, you may find yourself asking, does the scientific evidence behind the aerphobic life-style come from? The pioneering clinical research into aerphobics was carried out, and is still being advanced, at the Federated Aerphobics Training and Clinical Institute and Technological Yeshiva, known commonly to millions of Americans by the acronym FAT CITY. Founded by Dr. Melvin Practiss, dentist cum philosopher and author of the best-selling *Fat Is Beautiful* (Big, Brown & Co., $9.95), FAT CITY and its tax-exempt nonprofit research arm, the Sedentary Institute of Technology,[1] maintain two research centers in the United States. FAT CITY East is located at Port Lee, New Jersey, and FAT CITY West is housed in the MGM Grand Hotel in Las Vegas.

Using the latest technological advances (Cuisinarts, Fry-Babys, etc.), the institute carefully subjects selected research patients to a battery of physical examinations, exercise-deprivation, and intensive food-consumption. Only when clinically proven and statistically significant results have been

1. The Sedentary Institute of Technology is supported by grants from The American Beer Nut Board, Coronary Bypass Equipment Co., The North American Memorial Stone Council, More MSG Association, and others. Individual contributions are tax deductible and can be made payable to FAT CITY, Box LUNCH, Port Lee, New Jersey, or directly to Dr. Melvin Practiss, Villa Hefti, Rio-by-the-Sea-o, Brazil (in pounds, please).

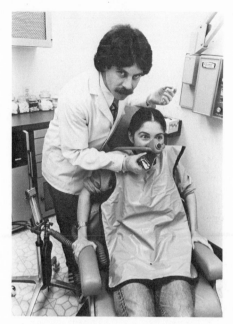

Dr. Al Zuckerman of Sedentary Institute administering
Devil Dog to chronic aerobe

obtained are these training techniques brought before the
general public.

Particular attention has been paid at the FAT CITY
clinics to the development of therapeutic programs for those
millions of Americans afflicted with the most severe symptoms of the virulent exercise epidemic. Both FAT CITY East
and FAT CITY West offer special Athlete De-Oxification
programs—week-long[2] sessions designed to break the athlete
of the exercise habit permanently. Sessions cost a mere
$1,000, and the cure rate among survivors is nearly 95
percent. The radical new techniques developed at FAT CITY
provide the basis for the common-sense therapies presented
in this book as a do-it-yourself way to stop exercising. You

2. Two-week fee is $1,450. With extra topping, $1,500.

may rest comfortably in the knowledge that whatever this book leads you to do, Dr. Practiss has done already, and made money at it.

HIGHLIGHTS OF SEVEN-DAY DE-OXIFICATION SCHEDULE

Day 1

8:30 A.M. Wake up

8:45 A.M. Weigh-in ceremony

9:00 A.M. Eggs Benedict Arnold (Canadian bacon, English muffin, french fries)

1:00 P.M.–1:10 P.M. Complete physical examination

4:00 P.M. Nap

7:00 P.M.–9:30 P.M. Dinner

12:00 P.M. Force-feeding

Day 2

9:00 A.M. Wake up

10:00 A.M. Breakfast in bed

1:00 P.M. Lunch in bed

5:00 P.M. Pastry bar opens

8:00 P.M. Luau—one pig to diner limit

11:00 P.M. Icebox-raiding expedition

Day 3 Salute to West Germany

9:30 A.M. Wake up

10:00 A.M. Breakfast: bratwurst-eating contest

1:00 P.M. Lunch: knackwurst-eating contest

2:00 P.M. Low tea: pastries, hot chocolate *mit schlag* (with feeling)

4:00 P.M. High tea: pastries, hot chocolate *mit schlag*

6:00 P.M. Cocktails: liverwurst-eating contest

7:00 P.M. First aid demonstration: Heimlich anti-choking maneuver, high colonics, intravenous Maalox administration

8:00 P.M. Bavarian beer hall orgy

Day 4

10:00 A.M. Wake up

11:00 A.M. Wake up again

11:30 A.M.–3:30 P.M. Brunch

4:00 P.M. Debate: Rolaids vs. Other Antacids: Learning to Consume 43 Times Your Own Weight

6:00 P.M.–8:00 P.M. Seventeen-course dinner: The Complete Cordon Bleu

9:30 P.M. Soufflé-sucking contest

Day 5

11:00 A.M. Wake up

11:30 A.M. Field trip: International House of Pancakes

2:00 P.M. Film: *Who's Killing the Great Chefs of Europe?*

2:15 P.M. Intermission

2:45 P.M. Intermission

3:15 P.M. Intermission

5:00 P.M. Clothes alterations

6:30 P.M.–6:30 A.M. Salute-to-Bacchus Buffet

Day 6

1:30 P.M. Wake up

2:00 P.M. Resuscitation

2:15 P.M. Brunch

3:15 P.M. Lunch

4:15 P.M. Munch

5:00 P.M. Belching lessons, snoring contest

7:00 P.M. Smorgasbord: Eat Your Weight

Day 7

3:00 P.M. Wake up

3:30 P.M. Eat everything not nailed down

4:00 P.M. Farewell speech. Tariff hike announcement by Dr. Practiss

4:30 P.M. Weigh-out ceremony—held at Highway Truck Weigh Station

8:30 P.M. Presentation of certificates to top achievers. Winners transported home by crane, ambulance.

The Twelve-Minute Aerphobic Check-up

Before undertaking any exercise program, a doctor's check-up is recommended. Beginning exercisers above the age of thirty are advised to take a stress electrocardiogram examination. In contrast, one of the beauties of the aerphobic regimen is that it requires no medical check-up.

A would-be beginner can check his or her aerphobic condition by means of a simple twelve-minute test:

- **Instructions.** Wear comfortable loose-fitting clothes, preferably a bathrobe or flannel nightshirt with slippers. Boxer shorts will also do (for both sexes). Sit in a well-padded armchair, with feet up on a stool, a six-pack of beer by your side. Ask a spotter to turn on the television and open the cans. Begin by chugging the six-pack with the dial set to "I Love Lucy" reruns. After twelve minutes, measure your physical state against the following chart of aerphobic fitness:
- **Lazy.** Belching, scratching. Throwing beer can at set when vertical hold fails.
- **Shiftless.** Motionless sitting, failure to remove empty beer can from lap. No reaction to vertical hold failure.
- **Indolent.** Beginning to nod off, head rolling, eyes glassy.
- **Slothful.** Head back, mouth open, loud snoring.
- **Comatose.** Body on floor, having fallen off chair. No vital signs evident.

AERPHOBIC CHECK-UP

Lazy phase

Shiftless phase

Indolent phase

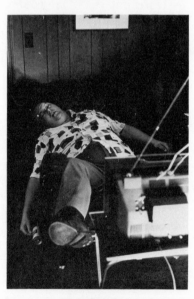

Slothful phase

Comatose-Peak physical condition

Do not be discouraged if, as a beginner, you do not even attain the first step (lazy) on this chart. But be aware that alertness, channel-switching, and set-adjusting are signs of serious physical and mental dysfunction. There are occasional reports of test-takers who shut off the set to exercise. These individuals should be forcibly restrained until professional help arrives.

The truly comatose state, the nirvana that all aerphobes seek, is beyond the initial grasp of the unlearned amateur. But after reading just a few chapters of this book you may find yourself displaying many of the symptoms associated with that esteemed condition.

Aerphobic Fitness Program

To achieve and maintain aerphobic conditioning, or "fatness fitness," a careful regimen of nonexercise must be maintained. The foundation of aerphobic fitness rests upon the twin pillars of rest and food, and to be aerphobically fit one must always strive to increase capacity for both.

A true aerphobicist is a well-rounded individual. "Round body, round mind," said the philosopher, planet, and Disney character Pluto. By gradually increasing both consumption and rest, anyone can achieve this well-rounded state in a matter of weeks.

"To sleep, perchance to dream," as a Great Dane once said, is among the noblest of life's ambitions. Most of us practice sleep daily; still, we often give up on sleeping after a mere six or eight hours each day. To become aerphobically fit, sleep-time must be increased. In time, and with the synergistic effect of systematic overeating, sleep-time can be doubled or even tripled. One is, in fact, limited only by the number of hours in a day. Beginners are advised to gradually augment their sleep-time, perhaps by napping, dozing off during work, or after dinner. Soon you will find yourself falling asleep with consummate ease—in elevators, while driving, or even during sex. But don't expect improvements overnight. Getting fit takes time, and the beginning sloth must weather fitful naps, brief reveries, and startling nightmares on the road to full-fledged narcolepsy.

A proper diet is as important as thorough rest. If,

indeed, we are what we eat, then the aerphobicist is the true modern man, eating every dish, crop, additive, and flavoring known to current technology. When the aerphobe isn't sleeping, he is eating. Most of us have traditionally—and foolishly—limited ourselves to three meals a day. Rather than eat to live, we must, as the advertising slogan has it, "live to eat." Again, start slowly if you are a beginning aerphobics practitioner. Nibbling leads quickly to snacking, snacking to noshing, noshing to fressing, gourmandizing, and ultimately, "pigging-out." A fourth meal late in the evening is a wise entrée to the world of overeating. Soon you will be ready to move on to a fifth, sixth, and so on until you reach the satiating *point-de-résistance*, where your waking hours have become one great sit-down meal.

To assist aspiring aerphobicists, the Sedentary Institute of Technology has devised an easy-to-follow scoreboard of our daily activities, rating them on an aerphobic point scale. Participants in the fitness program should strive to accumulate + 10 points every day, a + 3 being the minimum goal for beginners:

AERPHOBIC ACTIVITY SCALE

HOURS OF SLEEP (each one over ten a night)	+ 2
WALKING THE DOG	− 2
SHOOTING THE DOG	+ 1
LIFTING A SPOON	− 1
INTRAVENOUS FEEDING	+ 2
BREATHING	− 1
MEALS (each one over four a day)	+ 3
JOGGING	− 10
CROSS-COUNTRY SKIING	− 34
STANDING	− 2
STANDING ON LINE AT BASKIN-ROBBINS	+ 2
SEX WITH SPOUSE	− 3
SEX WITH OTHER(S)	− 7

SEX WITH SELF	−2
SEX WITH WHIPPED CREAM	+2
GROWING VEGETABLES	−6
EATING VEGETABLES	−1
EATING ANIMALS	+1
EATING ANIMAL CRACKERS (per Arkload)	+2
WALKING TO WORK	−4
RIDING TO WORK	−1
NOT GOING TO WORK	+1
TENNIS	−12
DOUBLES TENNIS	−7
DOUBLE SCOTCHES	+1

PART II

Aerphobics and the Exercise Problem

A Test for Exercise Addiction

Are you or is one near and dear to you suffering from a dependence on exercise? Often the afflicted (and those closest), are the last to know. But now, thanks to a simple ten-question test you can administer in your own home,[1] you can determine instantly your potential for addiction to workouts. Answer the following questions to the best of your ability, do not look at your neighbor's answers, and do not turn the page until you are instructed to do so. You may begin:

1. When you wake up at 7:00 A.M. do you:
   a. Go for a swim or jog.
   b. Shower for work.
   c. Go back to sleep.
2. When offered a piece of seven-layer cake, do you say:
   a. "No thanks. I'm in training."
   b. "Just a sliver."
   c. "Got any ice cream to go with it?"
3. Is your favorite fantasy:
   a. Winning the Tour de France, Boston Marathon, or swimming the English Channel.

1. Test for Exercise Addiction, Sedentary Institute of Technology, 1980. Copies of the official answer sheet are available by writing S.I.T. Test, Port Lee, New Jersey 01552. Enclose $59.95 for postage and handling.

    b. Sleeping with Raquel Welch or Robert Redford or both.

    c. Sleeping like Rip Van Winkle.

4. When people ask you your weight do you say:

    a. "A hundred and thirty, but I'm trying to drop another ten."

    b. "A hundred and sixty, but I keep meaning to try the Scarsdale Diet."

    c. "I dunno, the bathroom scale stops at two hundred and fifty."

5. When you buy footwear do you usually get:

    a. Adidas.

    b. Hush Puppies.

    c. Carpet slippers.

6. In winter do you:

    a. Cross-country ski.

    b. Wear galoshes to work.

    c. Hibernate.

7. When people ask what you do, do you say:

    a. "About five to ten miles a day."

    b. "——'s the name, ——'s the game."

    c. "I'm between jobs right now."

8. When you are thirsty do you prefer:

    a. A glass of fruit juice.

    b. A bottle of cola.

    c. A six-pack of beer.

9. On Sunday afternoon do you:

    a. Race.

    b. Visit friends or mow the lawn.

    c. Fall asleep during a football doubleheader.

10. Is your idol:

    a. Diana Nyad or Bill Rodgers.

    b. George Bush.

    c. Ed McMahon.

If you answered "a" to any of these questions, you are in need of immediate treatment. A "b" answer indicates that you show leanings toward an undesirable life of hard exercise and self-denial, but that hope still remains for your reclamation. If you answered "c," as the vast majority of American adults do, you are already on the aerphobic path to self-fulfillment. Congratulations and good night. The rest of you may now continue.

Aerobics Anonymous

A gaunt young man, his body wracked with emotion, stands before a smoke-filled room of friends, neighbors, and strangers. His testimony is familiar to the audience from other lips, but never from him, and telling it leaves him weak with sobbing gasps.

"I started two years ago. A friend of mine said, 'Try it, once around the park. You'll like it.' I did it, but I didn't feel much of anything, except sick. But we went out again the next night, and further that weekend. Before I knew it, I was doing ten to fifteen a day. It got so I couldn't go a day without an hour of it. Sometimes I'd get out of bed, and go off right then, before I even brushed my teeth. I lost forty pounds in two months. I had no appetite.

"It was hell for me, but I can't [sob] even imagine how bad it was for Marge and the kids. I was always out of the house, going around with a wild bunch. When I was home, I was either restless or asleep. I picked up on the slang, the clothes, the whole bit.

"It all ended the morning my wife gave birth to our son. The contractions were coming fast and she told me to go start up the car. I went outside, and it looked so nice, I went out to do my ten. I left her waiting, crying. Thank God the neighbors got her to the hospital. When I saw little Dougie I realized how crazy I had been [sob]. I quit, cold, and I haven't run a lap since."

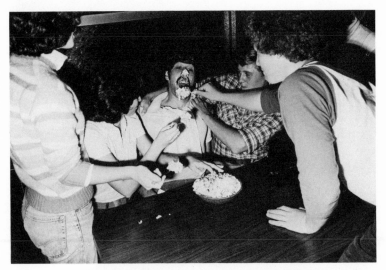

Addicted exerciser receives force feeding
(Soupy Sales method) at Aerobics Anonymous meeting

In bars, ice-cream parlors, and strip joints all around the country, scenes like this are being repeated daily. Addicted exercisers and ex-addicts are getting together over a double scotch, a banana split, or a silicone surprise, to discuss the agony of exercise. They are there of their own volition, as part of a new worldwide organization, Aerobics Anonymous.

With the support of the Sedentary Institute of Technology, which charges only minimal dues, new A.A. chapters have been springing up faster than disco roller rinks. The concept is a basic but effective one that has worked for drinkers, gamblers, and John Travolta fans. Just as these groups are subjected to horror stories of what too many margueritas, trips to the track, or Vinnie Barbarino jokes can do, so exercisers must confront the repercussions of their addiction.

The volunteer staff of cured exercisers is blunt, direct, but supportive. If an addict gets a sudden craving for a workout, he has only to call a hotline number, and an ex-

exerciser will be by his side in minutes to talk him down, pacify him with rich foods and stiff drinks, or even forcibly restrain him until the craze passes. It is a painful process, and not a pretty one, but through Aerobics Anonymous thousands of supposed incorrigibles have been saved.

Through your donations thousands more can be saved. So when the Aerobics Anonymous volunteer comes calling in his pink ice-cream truck, give and give generously.[1] The feet you save may be your own.

---

1. If you miss the wagon, you can pledge your donation during the annual Aerobics Anonymous Telethon, hosted this year by Stubby Kaye with poster-couple Jimmy Walker and Joan Rivers.

Swimming

The ability to swim is an instinct, one we, as other animals, acquired as a survival tool. It is therefore on a par as a "sport" with breast-feeding or sleeping.

From our earliest historical records we have evidence of man's hereditary ability to swim. Mosaics from Pompeii depict men dog-paddling in water,[1] but both the word and the recreational use of the ability to swim come from the early English. Until the nineteenth century when J. Trudgen introduced the aboriginal crawl to the West, the sidestroke and breaststroke were the predominant forms of staying afloat and in motion. There are now five basic strokes employed by swimmers:

1. *The front crawl.* The first stroke taught to youngsters, it is performed by alternating synchronized placement of hands and feet in a shuffling motion at the bottom of the pool. The head is lifted from the water for breath and cries of "ga-ga." This is most effective in the shallow end of the pool.
2. *The backstroke.* A relaxing stroke of alternating arm motions behind the head while lying chest up. In pools with concrete edges this often results in damage to back of head.
3. *The sidestroke.* An ineffective intermediary for those unable to choose between front and back or unable to correct spinning motion in the water.[2]

1. Apparently they didn't swim well in Pompeii.
2. One reason you don't see any Whirling Dervishes at Weekee-Wachee, or the ol' swimming hole for that matter.

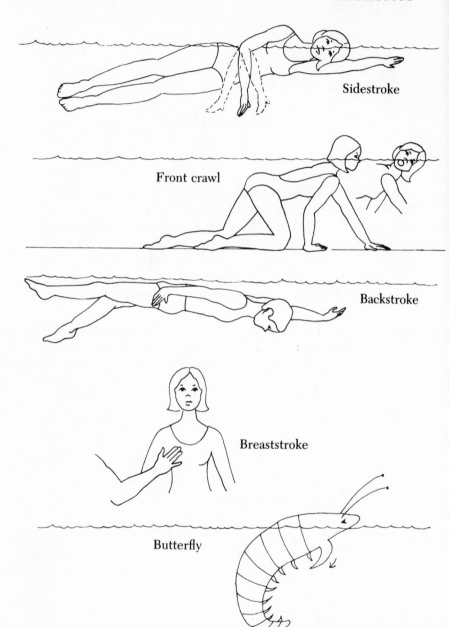

Sidestroke

Front crawl

Backstroke

Breaststroke

Butterfly

4. *The breaststroke*. A bit of sexual foreplay that has no place in swimming or a book on exercise.

5. *The butterfly*. A stroke popularized by small crustaceans.

For best results the swimmer dips him or herself in flour and bread crumbs before immersion in hot peanut oil (an exhausting technique).

Swimming and its companion activity, drowning, have long been popular pastimes, perverted from their transportory[3] functions. By and large, however, practitioners have refrained from the sort of exhausting distance swimming that characterized aerobic water sports. In salt water the effort is lessened by the buoyant effect of the mineral.[4] Swimming with river current is also a less offensive form, as are wading, body surfing, and the dead man's float.

How to stop swimming: To impede the aerobic misuse of our waters as an exercise medium, several simple public and private measures can be readily effected.

We must immediately have national legislation making swimming one-directional in all bodies of water including public swimming pools. One-way swimming will not inconvenience recreational pool users, but will prevent pool-bound aerobicists from completing more than a single lap. All but the most foolhardy of ocean swimmers will likewise be sidelined. Just to show our public broadmindedness, exercise-swimming will be permitted in whirlpools, waterfalls, Lake Erie, tidal waves, and bathtubs.

---

3. If it's not a word it should be.
4. If you live in Kansas or Paraguay you'll have to take my word for it.

Bicycling

Bicycling is a rather recent practice, the two-wheeler having been discovered in 1690 by the Frenchman De Sivrac, who somehow forgot the pedals. The rider pushed himself along. Not surprisingly, the idea never caught on.

In 1789 two other Frenchmen, Blanchard and Magurien, went De Sivrac one better and invented the tricycle. An Englishman named Johnson patented a push-yourself three-wheeler in 1818, but sales fell off sharply when it was discovered the exercise caused varicose veins.

Subsequent bicycles had larger front wheels than back, stylish modifications which caused a number of injuries. Maximum instability was achieved with the unicycle. The first two-wheelers brought to the United States were French wooden models with iron tires, referred to, accurately, as "bone-shakers."

In the 1860's rubber tires and wire spokes were invented, and in the 1880's the bicycle was popularized by the addition of pneumatic tires and even-sized wheels. Though the exact date is unclear the fad of bicycle-seat sniffing probably began at this time.

Bicycle racing became less popular when the automobile, a superior means of transportation, came into vogue. Bicycles survive only as recreational vehicles, except in Europe and Asia where people are still too illiterate to read highway signs or fill out registration renewals.

The promotion of bicycling as aerobic exercise and the

concurrent fad of European-made ten-speed bicycles have created a serious dollar drain on the American economy, particularly the Schwinn family. More than 100 million Americans now own bicycles, although recent studies have revealed that nine out of ten bicycles are sitting in the back of the garage next to the Flexible Flyer, gathering rust. Still the habit-forming risks of bike-riding as exercise cannot be underestimated. Particularly impressionable are the youngsters, lured onto handle-"bars" by shifty bike salesmen, or "pedal-pushers."

How to stop bicycle-riding: Bicycle riders must be made to understand the dangers inherent in using an antiquated means of conveyance in a modern age. To impress upon the rider the fragility and instability of the contraption, ask him or her to sit on the bicycle, feet on the pedals, without kickstand, and at a considerable distance from a supporting wall. After the rider has fallen to the side, step firmly on the wheel spokes.

Riding on sidewalks is widely illegal, so too is highway bicycling. The result is that coveys of cyclists consistently course city streets,[1] darting in between cars, and putting their muddy feet on your bumper. They may be cleansing their arteries but they are clogging the civic ones. Regrettably, the only way to stop these ruffians is to run them down, a feat that can be accomplished with only minimal damage to your paint jobs.

Running down cyclists can be a challenging and entertaining hobby, and is heartily recommended as a nontaxing aerphobic exercise. In addition, the activity has been endorsed by a number of taxicab organizations.

If the cyclist is aware that he has become a quarry he may initiate evasive maneuvers. Given the handling ability of the two-wheeler, you are off on a stiff test of driving skill, a

1. Say this last phrase three times quickly. Did you do it? Are you proud of yourself? Do you do everything books tell you to do?

A clean kill: Student body president awards the
helmet to expert driver

chase as satisfying as shooting the last tiger in the wild. Score
points for yourself according to quickness and cleanliness of
kill. If impressed, your fellow drivers may award you the
ears.

Less testing but equally important as a deterrent to the
exercise is *board-whomping*, a practice performed for de-
cades in that bastion of civility, the American Southwest.
From an open car window the unsuspecting bicyclist is struck
in the back with a two-by-four, known in France as a
dérailleur. The ensuing dive can be rated for form and
degree of difficulty.

These are harsh measures, but if we are to eradicate
these dope-pedallers, harsh measures are needed.

Running

About running, too much has been said already, so let us restrict ourselves to a cursory history of that ignoble exercise.

The human body was built to run, according to some anthropologists. The aerphobe knows that it is not running, but our capacity for thought or speech, and in a few cases the two together, which distinguishes us from lesser creatures. Horses are far better adapted for distance and sprint running than humans; yet with but one notable exception[1] no horse has mastered even the rudiments of everyday speech.

So much for prehistory. The onset of civilization was a direct outgrowth of our burgeoning mental, rather than physical, capabilities. Already, in the remains of the most primitive human settlements we see evidence of the human predisposition toward aerphobics. How else can one explain the presence of cooking and eating utensils and the complete absence of stop-watch fragments, or encrusted sweat suits in archaeological excavations?[2]

Among the great societies of history we see a social structure which all but precludes running. The Mesopotamian legal code was clearly detrimental to running; the eye-

1. One horse, of course, is known to have spoken in a smooth baritone, with an unfortunate preference for stale one-liners. The horse, which prefers to remain anonymous, is known in the literature by the pseudonym "Mr. Edward ——."
2. Author-archaeologist-car dealer Eric Von Danskin has hypothesized that giant alien athletes used Earth for track-and-field meets in ancient times, the Grand Canyon, for example, being a long-jump pit. For further data see *Invitational Games of the Gods* by E. Von Danskin, Pseudo Books, Atlantis ($9.95).

for-an-eye business probably led quickly to a foot for a foot.
The Egyptians were too busy at construction jobs.

The first aerobics practitioners were the Hebrews, who
spent forty years in motion, on a recommended low-fat, high-
matzoh carbohydrate diet. Even so, Jews to this day look
back on those years as ones of suffering, not useful conditioning, and wisely limit their matzoh consumption to one
week per year. The ancient Chinese apparently were heavily
into one-wall handball.

But the aerobic exercise of running did take hold in
ancient Greece, despite the sudden-death finish of the first
Marathoner, Phidippides. Still, since Olympic Games were
held in Olympia, only a hop, step, and jump across the
Pelopennessus from the rest of the known world, the sphere
of influence of running then cannot be compared to the
present.

After the fall of Greco-Roman civilization, running fell
once again into disfavor. The barbarians traveled by horse-
back, dismounting only for an occasional sack, plunder, or
snack of steak Tartare. Even the most well-read historical
scholar would be hard-pressed to name a halfway decent
Visigoth miler.

During the Dark Ages it was simply too dark to run; the
only things that were illuminated were the manuscripts.
Besides, the sharp angles of the cloisters made it impossible
to maintain any speed when running laps. While the West
was stumbling along in this feudal state, the Turkish star was
on the rise in the Middle East. Triumphant practitioners of
aerphobics, the Turks were a sedentary lot, and from their
lounging habits comes the name Ottoman Empire.

As the West revived, the Ottoman Empire became, as
history books so pejoratively proclaim, "moribund," a condition which persists to this day. This "moribund" state is in
reality an extension of the same blissful and degenerative
indolence which characterized the heyday of the Empire.
Meanwhile, the Renaissance—a rebirth of the arts, sciences,

The obedient runner . . .

. . . heads for trouble

and commerce, which clearly left everyone too tired to exercise—flourished in Europe. Leonardo da Vinci, who at one time or another made nonworking drawings for everything, devoted space to helicopters and tanks, but none to running shoes. Modern man was clearly grasping for something to move *him* around, a cornerstone of aerphobic philosophy. The Industrial Revolution provided the mechanisms to liberate us from physical exertion. The railroad, automobile, airplane, and hang glider—each in turn freed us further from the drudgery of peripateticism.

Thus, runners are willfully ignoring eons of evolution and centuries of history in which man has developed himself as well as his environment to make exercise unnecessary. It can only be hoped that the now better-informed will obey the lessons of history and so not be forced to repeat them. If this warning does not suffice, the runner may be induced to quit via the following historical method:

How to quit running: A half-hour before the scheduled jog, begin selected readings from the myriad books on running that are running over the shelves of bookstores. Fixx, Sheehan, Henderson, Costill, Van Aaken, and others will cause even the most dedicated runner to nod off. If and when the reader wakes up, it will be too late to run. *Warning:* Running literature is a powerful sedative and should not be administered without prescription.

Cross-Country Skiing

Without resorting to unfounded generalizations, it can be fairly stated that cross-country skiing is the poor man's downhill, a sport for those without the means or slopes to have a genuinely good time. While downhilling is a sociable sport, introducing the aficionado to a variety of bums, bunnies, and orthopedists, cross-country skiing is lonely drudgery.

Skiing has been around for thousands of years, the first skis having been used nearly 5,000 years ago in Scandinavia. The Nordic peoples have always been a restless, self-punishing sort, from Leif Ericson down to Ingmar Bergman. Not having the good sense to come in out of the snow, they invented flat bone skis to travel the countryside.

Only in Christian times was the wooden ski, nearly eight feet long, substituted. After some disastrous experiments with a downward-bent ski tip, the ski was curved upward to prevent impaling the neighbors' feet. Until the sixteenth century, wooden skis of this length, with strips of goat or sheepskin on the blades, were a hot number. Then the Swedes, who were warlike in addition to their other flaws, shortened the ski to three feet and made it into a combined ski-snowshoe, or "skoe." From this term the toast "skol" evolved, meaning literally, "get your ski off my foot."

Skiing was introduced into Central Europe in 1590, and spread rapidly to other godforsaken frozen climes. In 1840 Swedish immigrants brought the "wooden blade" to the

United States. By virtue of the activity's self-abusive nature, it dwelt in oblivion, except for the annual Dartmouth Carnival, until some bright post-World War I entrepreneurs had the sensible idea of creating the leisurely downhill-skiing business.

Cross-country skiing remained all but unknown until aerobics-minded exercisers of the last decade rekindled an interest in the activity as a tool for full body-conditioning. This is but another way of saying that cross-country skiing is an exhausting waste of time. By adding color coordinated knickers, lighted trails, fiber-glass skis, and more, devotees have made the "sport" nearly as expensive, if not as enjoyable, as downhill skiing. In typical aerobic fashion, a costly sport has been created from a primitive means of transportation.[1]

Cross-country ski slob waxes pathetic

1. Aerphobes assert that if you must go out in winter, take the snowmobile.

HOW TO STOP CROSS-COUNTRY SKIING: Blueberry waffles. A simple matter of olfactory deduction will bring you to this answer. Skiing is not much without snow; snow calls for cold weather. If you can't relocate south of the Mason-Dixon line or paint Saharan scenes on all the windows, you are going to need alternate means of waylaying the would-be skier on those occasional days when it is snowing but not storming, subfreezing but not frostbite inducing.

On such days it's still too cold for anyone in his right mind to leave the house, but even the most foolhardy aerobe will be sidetracked by the heady perfumes of flapjacks and coffee.[2]

As for skiers who prefer the technology of the last century and so wax their skis, you needn't bother to mess in the kitchen. By the time they've messed with grunewald, klisters, kicker waxes, and other paraffin-alia they will be literally stuck inside.

2. If you want to get rid of them try farina and eggnog.

Rope-Skipping

We cannot overlook rope-skipping as an aerobic exercise, try as we might. Jumping rope is considered to be one of the most efficient cardiovascular exercises; it is also one of the most mindless activities known to man, as the proficiency of boxers in this exercise demonstrates.

Since most of us over the age of six pay little mind to rope-skipping, it is not surprising that little is known about the origins of the curious behavior. After laborious research that spanned five continents, I uncovered a dog-eared copy of a manuscript of considerable historical significance, titled "On the Origins and Uses of the Jumping Strand" by Judge Ray "Jumping" Bean.

Judge Bean, brother of the infamous Wild West judge Roy Bean, was himself a law official in the early frontier days. I quote from his erudite text: "In my youth I was accustomed to endurance in wild sports, but never did I encounter a greater physical hardship than that which I witnessed while on expedition along the Congo River. I chanced upon a group of Mbutsi performing a ceremonial ritual Hicongo-Locongo, jumping to exhaustion over a llana of the genus *closelina*. I was forbidden to take part in this day-long ritual, blessedly. It appears to be a savage rite of passage for the prepubescent heathen. The sweat-drenched youngsters were apparently under some sort of spell, as they muttered continuously a

Rope-skipping demonstration by
Rocky Rhodes, middleweight
contender

Rocky's advanced maneuver

Rocky's last maneuver

phrase I transcribed as: 'Hutforent inquire with in, if I move outlett —— move in.'"[1]

Bean brought this custom back to the Tombstone Territory, as a torture for prisoners scheduled for execution, using the same rope with which the prisoner was later hanged. For many years rope-skipping prisoners provided warm-up entertainment for the bloodthirsty crowd.

Rope-skipping survived as a form of punishment visited largely upon young people here and abroad. A particularly brutal form, "Double Dutch," was imported from Holland. In England poorly toilet-trained infants were required to "skip to the loo."

Gradually, rope-skipping evolved into a children's game, a regrettable degeneration of tradition. But with the exception of the aforementioned addle-brained pugilists, rope-skipping was never thought of as a fitness-enhancing exercise for adults until the age of aerobics.

HOW TO STOP JUMPING ROPE: Do you really need to be told to stop? If you live in an apartment, the people downstairs probably will kill you if you don't. Think how silly you look. Think what happens to all things that go up, and to people who are given enough rope.

Even proponents of the jump-rope's physiological benefits find it difficult to defend or maintain an interest in rope-skipping. Hopping on two feet, skipping on one, turning the rope forward or backward; the creative possibilities are not exactly endless.

If there are indeed any confirmed rope-skippers around, there is little, short of moving them into a gerbil cage, that you can do to prevent them from jumping. So appeal to their desperate need for adventure by suggesting any of the following:

1. Reprinted by permission of S.I.T. Press, $3.95 (16 pages), cassette tapes $9.95.

1. Jumping rope while standing on your head
2. Jumping rope using a boa constrictor
3. Jumping rope on a tightrope
4. Jumping rope in the shower
5. Jumping rope with live wires (use rubber gloves—you trip, you lose)

Aerobic Dancing
(Including Disco)

This is an exercise? Sadly, it is, and a booming one. Aerobic dance clinics are sprouting up all over the land. Large exercise classes largely for large adult women, they stress regular and repeated dance motion as a means of cardiovascular and muscular conditioning. There are even two new books on the subject. Then again there are dozens of books on demonic possession, and you don't see many people signing up for that.

Yet the aerobic dance movement gains in popularity. It *is* convenient. A flat floor is all the equipment necessary, and several of those are found in just about every civilization. Unlike true dance studios, there are no mirrors required here, as students do not want reminding of their physical and terpsichoreal forms. Teachers are recruited from the ranks of former students and the whole affair is very social for the participants, and very profitable for the organizers. Pupils are charged a modest fee, for instruction in such advanced concepts as moving, stretching, and moving again.

Dance as an art form, a custom, and a form of entertainment existed for centuries before it was detoured into aerobic exercise. Dance is the universal human mode of expression. Bushmen dance on one foot in their huts.[1] New

1. One foot to a Bushman.

Caledonians wiggle in place. Fijians jump from side to side. Archie Bell and the Drells do the Tighten Up.

Unfortunately, the artistry of dance, which reached its peak as recently as the farewell appearance of Ramon and Yolanda on the "Ed Sullivan Show," has fallen into disrepute, subverted by aerobic exercise and promiscuous mating-dating dances (disco).

Disco is a contemporary cultural phenomenon closely related to aerobic dancing, in that participants lose all semblance of individuality. Hypnotized by a prescribed disco rhythm, disco-drones don the movement's polyester uniform—white three-piece suit for men, loud low-cut dresses and high heels for women. Discoers will often exercise for hours on end, breaking only long enough to open buttons, clear ears, pop pills, and dive into back seats. Such physical exertion is in itself clearly medically contra-indicated. Mental deterioration is also apparent; within a few weeks there are signs of strutting, Travolta-Summer fixation, and inability to converse beyond the basic "hey," "like wow," and "wanna dance?"

Disco is exhausting exercise. As the following chart, computed by S.I.T. engineers on location at Club Zippo in downtown Port Lee, indicates, the near constant and frenetic motions of disco are a highly virulent form of exercise. In calories expended per minute (CEM), disco dance rates on a par with the decathlon, swimming the Hellespont, or having the plague. Ranked by S.I.T. in regard to other dance forms, the results are similarly depressing:

DANCE	CALORIES EXPENDED PER MINUTE
The Freak	577.75
The Horah	543.09
Whirling Dervishes	533.78
The Bump	479.78

DANCE	CALORIES EXPENDED PER MINUTE
Charleston	455.32
Latin Hustle	442.13
Lindy	289.05
The Freddy	154.43
Virginia Reel	58.57
Gavotte[2]	46.65
The Stroll	36.76
Fox Trot	34.43
Cake Walk	17.78
Sleepwalk	6.67

HOW TO STOP DANCING THROUGH AERPHOBICS: The best time to stop dancing, as Orson Bean probably would like to have said, is before you beguine. In the words of noted hoofer Groucho Marx, "Take a rumba from one to ten." And sit down.

As an aerphobe the most effective way you can stop someone from dancing is to be his or her partner. It's a sacrifice, admittedly, to hit the dance floor. But one day your footloose aerobic friend will thank you for it. That is, when he or she is all healed.

Dancing with you, your aerobic partner will immediately notice that the pace has slowed, the floor space narrowed. Pressing closer still, you can impress your aerphobic physique on your partner's feet.[3] After just a few moments of unfamiliar exercise, you will have used up most of the available oxygen in the room, and your hot breath and

2. A more sophisticated form of "Oi Gavolt."
3. Or more in the case of the Bump.

A fatal case of disco fever

fetid body odor will give even the most devout disco-conut a terminal case of Saturday Night Ague.

As for your aerobic dancing friend, give her a leotard and a full-length mirror. After all, what are friends for? One disheartening glance in the glass, and she'll need your broad shoulder to cry on all the way to Howard Johnson's.

The Beginner

The best time to stop exercising is, of course, before you start. Aerobicists, under various pretenses, will be beseeching you to try their favorite form of torture so that they will not be alone in their misery. This proselytizing is motivated by the same feelings that Mencken noted in Puritans, who lived in mortal fear that someone, somewhere was having a good time.

Aerobics is addictive and it, like all strenuous activity, is to be avoided. There are countless horror stories of middle-aged housewives, older men, even young children, who are seduced into a Sunday afternoon "fun-run," "bike-a-thon," or swim meet, only to end up as ten- to twenty-mile-a-day activity-addicts. Here is a profile of one such beginner, drawn from the S.I.T. file of exerciser case-histories:

PATRICIA CAKE—age 37—height 5'2"—weight 145 lbs. The chunky brunette mother of five lives with her family in Faker Heights, Ohio. Ms. Cake last participated in an athletic activity when she was a Brownie, and has been confined to driving in a ten-mile radius of her home since 1964. Ms. Cake decided to start exercising one month ago when her youngest son compared her unfavorably to the Goodyear blimp. Ms. Cake chose bicycling after it was recommended by Rachel on "Another World." Her first tours were from the kitchen door to the mailbox, but she now cycles a full mile in slightly less than an afternoon.

Patty Cake dressed to cycle

HOW TO STOP THE BEGINNING EXERCISER: To help the beginner, such as Ms. Cake, resist the exercise procurer, here is a convenient list of deterrent phrases, in declining order of preference, devised by the researchers at S.I.T.

1. *(Psychology)* "I'll go with you, but don't expect more than fifteen miles from me today."
2. *(Nuisance)* "Can we stop at the store on the way?"
3. *(Ennui)* "Could you just wait with me until 'Hollywood Squares' is over?"
4. *(Offensiveness)* "Mind if I wear my good-luck garlic necklace?"
5. *(Extreme offensiveness)* "Should I? I've been eating prunes all day."
6. *(Physiology)* "Gee, I'd love to, but I hyperextended my achilles tendon yesterday."

7. *(Alternate obsession)* "No, but how about a few ———."

8. *(Craziness)* "I'd love to, but it's a bad day for Libras."

9. *(Danger)* "I can't leave the house, there's a hit man after me."

10. *(Insult)* "With you, ha!"

The Expert

At the opposing end of the exercise scale[1] from the beginning
exerciser is the confirmed aerobicist: the five-mile-a-day
swimmer, ten-mile runner, or fifty-mile biker. A representative case history from the S.I.T. files exemplifies the typical
chronic exercise-user:

MILES STANDOFFISH—age 32—height 6'2"—weight 131 lbs.
A former high-school swim-team standout, Standoffish was a
successful and gregarious computer software salesman and
infrequent municipal-pool visitor until his late twenties. But
after participating in a weekend encounter marathon-hot-tub
soak sponsored by the Exercise Transcendentalist Workshop
in Essalen, California, Miles quit his $30,000 Boston job and
"splat for the Coast." Standoffish swims fifteen miles each
morning and runs ten in the evening, and does three hours of
yoga daily, which leaves only enough waking time to shower,
shave, and brush his upper teeth. He eats only bee pollen,
fasts on days with a *T* in them, and supports himself selling
hashish he grows hydroponically in his trunks. Standoffish
holds the California 10,000-meter swim record for hippies
over thirty and is now recovering from his fourth operation to
correct chronic skin-puckering.

HOW TO STOP AN ENDURANCE ATHLETE: Conventional
appeals to adopt the rational sedentariness clearly have no

---

1. Or any scale for that matter.

effect on hardened aerobicists such as Standoffish. Even psychological reconditioning[2] may have little effect on these exercise addicts. But one method remains:

Invite the exerciser in question to participate in an endurance event which you have organized. As the racer approaches each checkpointed intersection in the race, direct him or her away from the race route. As only the one swimmer, jogger, cyclist, or skier will be so misdirected, he or she will be convinced that he or she is in the lead, and so press on at a fast pace.

Post mileage markers along the detour route which grossly underestimate the actual distance covered. A circuitous route of some 140 miles can be labeled as 26 miles, and the athlete, thinking him or herself to be disoriented by the excitement, will push on. The veteran competitor will be loath to give up short of completion of the race and will eventually become so fatigued as to collapse. At this time the

Dejected marathoner watches life pass him by

2. A.k.a. behavioral modification. See *Manchurian Candidate* for swimmers.

victim is to be brought by stretcher to a point along the actual race route and revived to witness late-finishing oldsters, kids, and lesser physical specimens. The exerciser will be demoralized by the sight of these slobs finishing when he or she could not.

The combined physical and psychological effects have been known to prompt some aerobicists to turn to checkers, crocheting, and corporate law, to name a few A-rated aerphobic activities.

PART III

Exercise and the Aerphobic Body

Exercise and Sex

The potentially catastrophic effects of exercise on sex are not widely known.

Successful sex during aerobic exercise is extremely rare, requiring a high degree of accuracy and flexibility. Partners must synchronize length of speed, stroke, and stride to "pull it off," in the best sense of the phrase. Foreplay is a somewhat easier matter to accomplish, provided the athletes are able to keep abreast. If partners are not of approximately the same size and level of ability, biking, swimming, skiing, or running sex can cause a variety of injuries in affected areas ranging from chafing—which skiers can prevent by using their wax—to dislocation and stress fractures. The would-be lover-exerciser is further advised that the experience is nearly always frustrated in the end by the unavailability of a post-coital cigarette.

More insidious are the long-term sexual injuries which befall the individual exerciser and can affect sexual function. For well-endowed members of either sex, the constant yo-yoing effect of aerobic exercise, particularly rope-skipping, can result in unsightly and uncomfortable lengthening of the sexual organs. Unless restraining devices are worn, these participants may seriously injure themselves or their sexual partners. While performing the exercise, such individuals are well advised to wear restraining devices, such as are readily available in attractive colors, styles, and materials at your local bondage-and-dominance outlet. Without such precautions sudden stops may produce a painful whiplash effect.

Exercise can have quite the opposite effect upon less-developed individuals. Weight loss and increased muscular tone conspire, metaphorically, to push the peas back in the pod. Many veteran exercisers report significant decreases in penile length after strenuous workouts.[1]

CORRELATION CHART—EXERCISE TO SEX

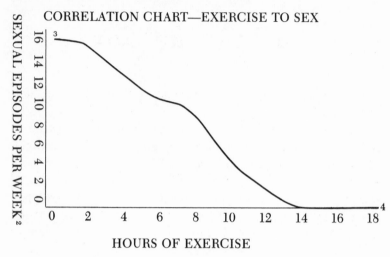

HOURS OF EXERCISE

Sex is an infinitely more productive and pleasurable exercise than running. It can also be an effective aerphobic substitute for running, when used in a conscientiously applied program of oral hygiene and regular professional care. As methadone simulates heroin, so sex simulates many of the physical effects that exercise causes: sweating, soreness, and a feeling of lassitude upon termination. Like marathoners, successful sexual athletes report the sensation of "hitting the wall" after much exertion, a point beyond which they can continue only by sheer willpower or crowd stimulus.

Unlike exercise, however, sex produces few serious injuries and is not habit forming. In fact, most couples report a sharp decline in the number of sexual encounters after the initial year.

Sex is even cheaper and more accessible than aerobic

1. See the aptly named Frank Shorter.
2. This does not refer to "Charlie's Angels" shows.
3. Aerophobic fatness fitness.
4. Aerobic fitness.

activity. It can be performed in any weather, in water, on land, or in the air, and it requires no special equipment.[5] If

A healthy bit of sexercise

you wish to try a sex-substitution program to stop exercising, the following recommendations will be of assistance.

How to stop exercising through sex: The aerphobicist must discipline him or herself to have sex whenever the desire to work out becomes overpowering. Maintain good training habits, using these eight steps as a guide:

1. Don't eat spicy foods before, during, or immediately after.

2. Dress appropriately (no hats).

3. Don't rush. Remember: finishing first is not necessarily winning.

4. Do warm-ups—they are essential to preventing injury.

5. Form a support group to sexercise together. Spurred on by others you will go farther.

6. Don't vary your pace suddenly.

7. Don't let an opportunity to sexercise escape, whether at home, work, or in between.

8. Don't ever say you have a headache.

Warning: Don't mix oysters, quaaludes, saltpeter, and Spanish fly.

5. For special equipment and group functions call Mildred (TY7-803).

Exercise and Diet

Running proponents frequently cite the evidence of long-lived peoples in areas where cardiovascular exercise via running or skiing in high-altitude surroundings is *high,* and consumption of food, particularly fat, is *low.* The Hunzas of the Asian highlands lead long and active lives, subsisting on a diet of apricots and fermented dairy products. The fundamental question begged by such a regimen, is whether such a life, no matter how long, is worth living. Are the Hunzas just desperately hanging on in hopes of a decent cheeseburger? The answer, if I may put words into their atrophied mouths, is "yes!"[1]

Exercise itself has been shown to suppress appetite and so deprives us of one of the few genuine pleasures in life. Exercisers can't eat after workouts or during, and they avoid eating before them. Exercisers frequently espouse the theory that the standard weight recommendations for Americans[2] are ten to twenty pounds high, a sorry bit of rationalizing in defense of their own wasted physiques. When runners do eat, they shun calorie-rich foods, meaning nearly everything that tastes good, and the result is a growing minority of Don Knotts look-alikes.

Unfortunately, the aerobicist's obsession with losing weight has struck a sensitive nerve among many regular folk

1. Pronounced "yess" in Hunzarian.
2. As determined by the Council of Physicians and Coin-Operated Scale Vendors (CPCOSV).

who have taken up exercise or a combined exercise and diet program to achieve weight loss. But we know a mile of running consumes only 100 calories, or one thirty-fifth of a pound. If one feels the misguided impulse to diet, 100 calories could be lost in a far less painful and time-consuming manner, by not eating one banana. Not eating seven ice-cream sundaes each day could mean a weight loss of twenty pounds in just a week. The most extreme form of this abstemious regimen is the Scarsdale Diet, in which you may prepare an unlimited portion of carefully selected foods, provided you give the entire meal to your servants. Such diets are not only in violation of the Geneva Accords Against Torture, they are unnecessary, as aerphobics shows us.

Aerphobics teaches us to accept ourselves as we are, fat and logy, and not to strive for anorexic dimensions. Body fat has a number of benefits. It is "nature's fiber-glass insulation,"[3] keeping us warm, an especially valuable function in these times of harsh winters and rising fuel costs. Fat shields our precious bodily organs from injury, providing a shock-proof bumper for all of life's elbowings, bumpings, and head-on collisions. A gram of fat contains twice the energy potential of a gram of protein or carbohydrate, and our fat stores are insurance against sudden drought, famine, fudge shortage, or other catastrophe.

If more of the world's poor took the precaution of becoming fat, they would not suffer so from famine. Should a worldwide food shortage occur, it is not the meek who will inherit the earth but the chubby, and so we can take comfort in the knowledge that no nation is more secure than our own.

3. From "I am Joe's Adipose," *Reader's Digest*, May, 1954.

IDEAL WEIGHT TABLES

WOMEN

Height	Standard Weight	Aerobic Ideal Weight	Aerphobic Ideal Weight
4'10"[4]	85	81	150
4'11"	92	88	162
5'0"	99	92	173
5'1"	106	98	184
5'2"	112	103	191
5'3"	118	108	204
5'4"	123	112	217
5'5"	128	116	232
5'6"	134	121	248
5'7"	139	125	264
5'8"	144	129	281
5'9"[5]	148	133	300

MEN

Height	Standard Weight	Aerobic Ideal Weight	Aerphobic Ideal Weight
5'4"[6]	120	112[7]	184
5'5"	128	118	191
5'6"	135	124	200
5'7"	150	136	212
5'8"	153	139	222
5'9"	160	142	234
5'10"	166	147	246
5'11"	173	152	258
6'0"	180	159	271
6'1"	188	163	290
6'2"	195	169	314

4. If you are under this height, nobody much notices how much you weigh.
5. If you are taller than this, you can weigh whatever you damn please.
6. In the case of aerphobics, width.
7. Note weights here identical for 5'4" man and 5'4" woman. Thus, this is the ideal height for those contemplating transsexual operations.

The numbers of overweight amongst us testify to the superiority of the aerphobic philosophy. So too does a sample aerphobically balanced diet[8] when contrasted with a representative rabbit-food scrap sampling from a health-conscious exerciser.

EXERCISER'S HEALTH FOOD	AERPHOBIC SUBSTITUTE
yogurt	ice cream
wheat germ	pistachio nuts
bran	chocolate sprinkles
orange juice	scotch
lentils	sirloin steak
cottage cheese	whipped cream
raisins	chocolate kisses
brown rice	fettucini alfredo
miso	baklava
tamari	mousse au chocolat
tahini	Black Forest cake
apple(s)	apple pie(s)
banana	banana split
vitamins	additives
minerals	preservatives
no eating out	eat anytime, anywhere except parts of Cambridge, Berkeley, Ann Arbor, and Greenwich Village

8. A "balanced" diet is one in which the weight of each food eaten is identical, i.e., a one-pound steak calls for one pound of ice cream to follow.

One day's food for aerobe

Aerphobic light snack

SAMPLE DAILY DIET

Exerciser	Aerphobicist
7:30 A.M. *Breakfast*. Juice, whole wheat cereal, herb tea	8:00 A.M. Simulated bacon strips, three fried eggs, pancakes with margarine and imitation syrup, white toast with grape jelly, two cups coffee with equal amounts of artificial creamer and sugar
10:00 A.M. Glass of cider	10:00 A.M. Coffee, jelly donuts
12:30 P.M. *Lunch*. Low-fat plain yogurt, cantaloupe half, celery tonic	12:30 P.M. Bologna sandwiches, french fries, malted, Ring-Dings
2:00 P.M. Glass of spring water	2:00 P.M. Coffee, candy bar
	4:00 P.M. Coffee
6:30 P.M. *Dinner*. Bean sprout salad, brown rice, steamed vegetables, kefir	6:30 P.M. Soup, steak, mashed potatoes, canned beans, rolls, butter, chocolate cake, coffee
	10:30 P.M. Potato chips, Twinkies, beer
TOTAL CALORIES—543	TOTAL CALORIES—7,450

HOW TO STOP EXERCISING THROUGH DIET: The foregoing tables speak for themselves.[9] The evidence they present should suffice to deter the misguided would-be exerciser-dieter, but a more elaborate strategy is required to reorient the practicing aerobic noneater. You may wish to try "Carbohydrate Free-Loading" as a therapy.

Carbohydrate Free-Loading is a technique which requires extensive community cooperation and plays upon the distance athlete's practice of storing up on carbohydrate-rich foods in the days immediately preceding a race.

Begin by learning the exerciser's route for the last days of practice before a race. Ask neighbors in the line of flight to begin cooking pancakes at the appropriate time. Invitational yells of "get 'em while they're hot" are often helpful. After just one, or at most, two, such free-lunch stops the consumer will be too bloated to continue. In urban ethnic areas, such as Boston's North End, pasta may be successfully substituted.[10]

A second more technological means of waylaying the exerciser with food involves the use of the newly devised portable drink-dispensers. Porta-Snort[11] is a backpack-mounted battery-powered unit designed to supply users with liquid refreshment via a plastic hose as they move about. It should be easy to convince the practiced distance swimmer, runner, or skier, of the utility of such a device, as all are obsessed with fears of performance problems caused by fluid loss, and dehydration-induced electrolyte imbalances.

To be an effective running-deterrent, the standard Porta-Snort mixture of Gatorade and water must be mixed with equal parts of grain alcohol.[12] As the subject exercises and stimulates circulation upon an empty stomach, the

9. They say, "Don't eat that low-cal crap." (Tables are notoriously blunt.)
10. The weekly runs of Anthony Martinelli, terminated by spaghetti-loading, have been recorded on film.
11. Porta-Snort is marketed by Barrymore Enterprises, and costs $39.95. It may be ordered by writing BOX YOUR EARS, Port Lee, New Jersey.
12. Wood alcohol, or for that matter, molten lead, has more immediate and lasting effects.

alcohol injection will have an immediate and pronounced effect. The effort itself will soon terminate in a fit of laughter, tears, or nausea. In urban areas Porta-Snort–equipped runners and bikers can be easily tracked to the nearest bar, and in rural zones they seldom stray far from the first ditch into which they fall.

CORRELATION CHART—MEALS TO SLEEP

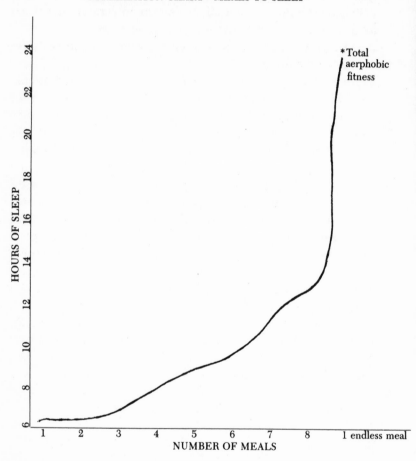

Courtesy of Sedentary Institute of Technology, Port Lee, New Jersey.

A far more direct and long-term solution to the exercise affliction is through total-immersion eating. Addicts are habitually careful to avoid eating within two hours of a scheduled workout because of the stitches, cramping, and nausea which often result. The obvious cure suggested by this behavior is to serve meals more frequently than every two hours. Allowing for a sating twelve-hour sleep, this entails no fewer than six full meals per day. After but a few weeks on the six-meal-a-day plan, the aerobicist will have attained proportions such that movement of any kind, not to mention endurance exercise, will be impossible.

Exercise and Warm-ups

Exercisers are frequently reminded to do preparatory limbering and stretching exercises by doctors who are aware of the risk of muscle-pulls and strains from the exercise. Despite yoga, calisthenics, and the like, the uneven stresses and incomplete nature of the activity frequently leave practitioners with such tight muscles in the back of their legs that they cannot pick up a coin without lying down next to it.

HOW TO STOP RUNNING THROUGH WARM-UPS: Inda Gudal-Summahtyme, author of *Yoga for Materialists* (O Press, New Delhi, .35¢), recommends the following exercises, originally taught to the British by Sepoy soldiers many years ago. The result of each of these is slow, but total, incapacitation:

The lion. Lie down on stomach, bring left leg up and over head to rest on ear. Grip hair with both hands. Pull. Place right leg in mouth to muffle screams.
The dog-owner. Stand. Bring left foot up to nose. Sniff. Bend backward and bite right calf sharply. Scratch all over.
The cat-owner. Lie down. Dig nails of left hand into neck, and across to eye. With right hand remove hairs from mouth and body. Kick forward with left foot, knocking over valuables.
The mating mantis. Lie on chest. Bring legs over back and head into mouth. Bite off legs.
The Gordian knot. Sit on hill with legs crossed. Place left arm

Dog-owner

Lion

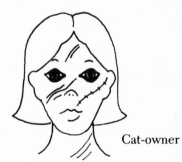

Cat-owner

Mating mantis

Gordian knot

Walk in New York

Quarterback

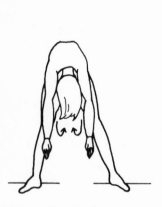

Big Fool

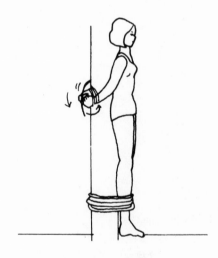

The Joan Crawford

through legs and up to grasp neck. Wind right arm through left arm, pass it through legs, and grip waist from behind. Roll.

The New York walk. Stand on left leg with right leg extended forward in ambulatory gait. Turn head backward, open mouth. Place knife against neck. Twist arms behind back. Scream.

The quarterback. Bend right knee inward, left knee out. Thrust stomach back, chest to side, and hips in opposite direction. Push head up and to side. Knock front teeth out with fists. Continue to stretch until wrenching sound is heard in legs.

The big fool. Stand naked with legs spread. Bend forward at the waist, bringing head between legs. Lift head and look into nearest opening.

The Joan Crawford. Bind hands, legs to pole. Place in 350° oven for two hours, turning to baste.

Exercise and Form

There isn't a hell of a lot of specialized skill involved in aerobic exercise. But if other authors can devote a chapter to it, so can we.

Aerobicists, regardless of the exercise, move with alternate strides of their feet or arms, or both. According to a $447,000 S.I.T. survey commissioned by the U.S. Department of Education, 64 percent of all exercisers begin moving with their left limb, 24 percent with their right, with 12 percent undecided.

Before exercising, every accomplished aerobicist calculates his maximal stride length, computed by dividing the length of the limbs into body weight in grams, and multiplying by a factor 3.14 times the radius of the joint in hectares. You may wish to perform this calculation in your head before setting off. This motion and stride length is to be maintained, except in areas where German shepherds abound.[1]

While the required motion for each exercise varies, the overall effect sought—one of lightness and relaxed bounce—is the same. To further this light feeling, aerobic swimmers, joggers, cyclists, and skiers wear thin clothes, and frequently shave their heads and pull out their toenails, fillings, and eyelashes to reduce drag.[2]

---

1. Greek shepherds are less messy.
2. False eyelashes, with the right dress, increase drag for some men.

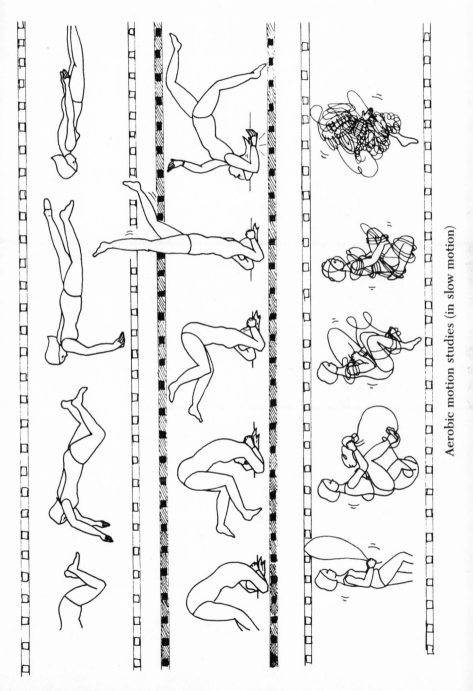

Aerobic motion studies (in slow motion)

HOW TO STOP EXERCISING THROUGH FORM: Take a home movie of the afflicted exerciser in motion.[3] No matter how much a novice he or she is, the imagined fluidity and rapidity of motion will be shockingly contradicted by the film. Now suggest the following radical changes in exercise style to your demoralized audience:

1. Count the number of strides or strokes. Result—paralyzing boredom.

2. Ski backward off the roof. Result—paralyzing paralysis.

3. Run without bending your knees.[4] Result—arrest for vagrancy.

4. Swim in an empty pool. Result—third-degree abrasions.

5. Bicycle with feet in the spokes. Result—sliced corned beef.

6. Work out with hands inside pants. Result—arrest for moral turpitude.

3. Slow motion if possible.
4. Also known as lurching.

COMPUTING OPTIMAL STRIDE LENGTH

BODY WEIGHT/LIMB RATIO[5]	1.7	2.3	3.0	3.7	4.4
2.19	4.54	4.22	.6	4.5	9.1
3.85	5.33	3.43	0	3.4	5.55
8.34	null	.54	4.5	3.2	7.0
7.46	1.14	6.7	5.3	1.5	8.9[6]

JOINT RADIUS IN HECTARES[7] (hrp)

The above is a simple computation, developed by Pentagon press officials—which you may perform with a home slide rule, abacus, or PDP-11 computer—to determine optimal stride length for a person of your body weight, limb length, and joint size.

5. Measured in body/limb inverse mass potential ("blimps").
6. Occasionally longer on horse-traveled routes.
7. Measured in hectare radical points ("herpees").

Exercise and Injuries

Exercise, fortunately for the rest of us, has a way of eventually doing in its participants, much like Russian Roulette. In particular a number of injuries befall the foot, and because of improper foot structure, the other parts of the body.[1] So, injuries such as lower back spasms, hip bursitis, chondromalacia patella (runner's knee), and shin splints are as much a product of exercise stress as bruised heels, plantar fasciitis, tendon pulls, and assorted sprains and strains.

Each aerobic sport carries its own special chronic-use injuries, from runner's knee to swimmer's ear, to the lesser-known but equally disabling skier's finger (from cutting skin on the edge of wax tins) and rope-jumper's wrist. Bicycle-riders run the highest risk of injury, and a terminal ailment called Chevrolet-in-the-face is quite common.

Of course, certain human physiological characteristics give rise to injury. People with one leg shorter than the other, such as the mountain-dwelling Swiss, are particularly prone to injury.[2] So too are those lacking in sinovial fluid to lubricate grinding joints.[3] Individuals who fail to do limbering exercises for moving muscles, and strengthening ones for their antagonist groups[4] are more prone to muscle pulls and strains. Bowlegged, flat-footed, or knock-kneed people—in

1. The knee bone is connected to the thigh bone, etc.
2. How else do you think they keep from tumbling down hills?
3. A lube job every 10,000 miles is recommended.
4. Even muscles have enemies.

short, all of us—may experience extreme unbalanced stress leading to injury from aerobic exercise. The most esoteric indicator of eventual damage is found in those people having second toes longer than their big toes,[5] a condition known as Morton's Foot. If you have Morton's Foot, you should by all means give it back.[6]

Since most exercisers are too stubborn to quit over minor things such as agonizing pain and disabling injury, a whole new field of sports medicine has evolved to treat the injured exerciser. Foremost among these medical specialists is the podiatrist, a practitioner whose status is only slightly above proctologist at the bottom of the specialist pile. It may well be that the aerobics movement was sponsored by podiatrists, who formerly had nothing else to do but cauterize an occasional plantar wart.

How to stop exercising through injury: The best way to stop exercising may be to keep at it. When it hurts to work out, work out some more. With such tenacity and fortitude, you will soon be living in traction or a Jacuzzi.

To augment the already considerable risk of injury from these exercises, you might try the following techniques:

1. Wear oxfords or high heels and ankle weights.
2. Swim in water with the highest mercury content.
3. Alternate right and left shoes or skis.
4. Run, ski, or bike ride in the middle of the street, always against traffic and always at rush hour.
5. Reverse your breathing pattern. Inhale under water or, when on land, do not inhale at all.

5. If you have only a big toe, you are probably a horse.
6. Courtesy of Henny Youngman's Used Jokes, Inc.

Exercise and Physiology

A wide range of beneficial bodily effects are claimed for aerobic exercise, from heart attack prevention to the disappearance of varicose veins.

The effects of these activities on weight loss, sexual activity, and brain function are discussed elsewhere in this book. But by far the strongest claim made for the fad's physiological benefits concerns its circulatory effects. In selectively stressing that system it is thought that exercise makes the heart beat more slowly, steadily, and efficiently, and the blood supply more widespread and oxygen-rich.[1] Involved are myoglobin exchange with arterial hemoglobin at the cellular level, capillary development, and lowered systolic and diastolic pressure. Gibberish? Of course.

Doctors, like aerobicists, enjoy using jargon to confuse and alienate the uninitiated. But thanks to the folks at S.I.T. we now have a common-sense, plain English guide explaining the role of exercise in circulation.[2] This excerpt from the manual should suffice:

> *Blood*, like electrical current, flows from the *heart*, or generator. It is carried by the *arteries*, red licorice-like cables, to the other *organs*, or main outlets in the body's house. A series of

1. Which should make them happy in Transylvania, at least.
2. From "A Plain English Guide Explaining the Role of Exercise in Circulation." Published by S.I.T. Press ($1.95, 22 pages).

THE HUMAN MACHINE

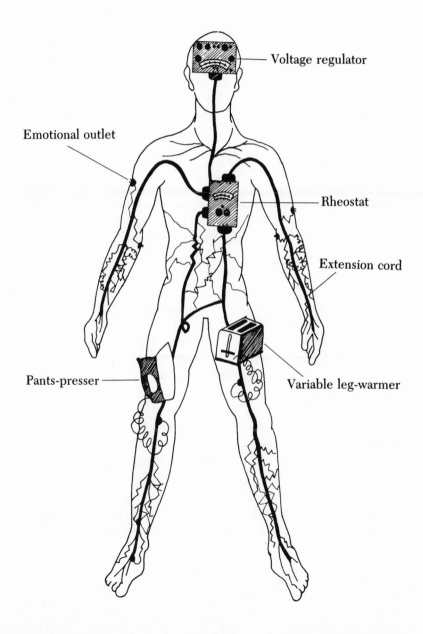

smaller *capillaries,* little wires, brings the "juice" to the *skin* and *extremities,* the extensions and appliances. In everyday life, calling for few *stresses,* or amperes, the generator operates smoothly.

But when you exercise, get scared, or are badly injured, your *nervous system,* the control panel, calls down for more "juice." Of course, there is always the risk that your wires may be frayed (age), crossed (fatigue), rusted (arteriosclerosis), or that you may have had too many outlets plugged in (overweight, alcoholism, etc.). Then the added demands of running can cause you to blow a fuse (heart attack) or conceivably short-circuit the whole system (bye-bye). A lighter load (diet, rest) and repair by a trained electrician (coronary bypass) may set you right again, but you are going to have stiff electric bills to pay.

So conserve energy.

HOW TO STOP EXERCISING THROUGH PHYSIOLOGY: Though the effects are by no means conclusively documented, most exercisers think they are warding off the threat of coronary troubles. Regular exercise is known, however, to produce so-called T-wave motion, heart irregularities which register on electrocardiogram readings.

Train the exerciser to recognize a normal electrocardiogram. This may take months, given the poor soul's limited attention span and atrophying mental skills. Then show him his own abnormal EKG. He should be sufficiently troubled to drop the sport, retire prematurely, and move to Arizona. A little knowledge is, indeed, a dangerous thing.

If this fails to make the necessary dent in the exerciser's skull, substitute any one of the following graphs for his or her EKG reading:

1. A whale song

2. Seismograph readings of the San Francisco Earthquake

3. A diagram of the Six Flags Amusement Park's roller coaster

4. This month's Dow Jones Averages. *Warning:* The shock may be fatal.

ELECTROCARDIOGRAMS — Interspecific Comparisons

HUMMINGBIRD

FLEA

CHIPMUNK

AEROBIC EXERCISER

DOG

SNAKE

SLOTH

SNAIL

AERPHOBE

CANTALOUPE

ELECTROCARDIOGRAMS — Intraspecific Comparisons

SAMMY DAVIS, JR.

HOYT WILHELM

EVEL KNIEVEL

RICHARD NIXON [3]

DOLLY PARTON [4]

BURT REYNOLDS [5]

JACQUES COUSTEAU

GENERAL
   CHIANG KAI-SHEK

3. Unexplained eighteen-second lapse.
4. Obligatory Dolly Parton joke.
5. Equal time provision for crass women.

Exercise and Drugs

The quest of the coveted "exercise high" is a powerful motivation behind the exercise movement's popularity. Scientists have now determined that exercise does indeed trigger the release of epinephrine, a booster shot of adrenaline that elevates the heart beat, performance, and mood of the participant, much as amphetamines do. In other words, exercisers are, knowingly or not, nothing more than "speed freaks."[1] Like upper-poppers they are restless, jumpy, and emaciated.

But, unlike drugs, exercise is, at least for now, legal in this society. Until we have the laws, and the get-tough enforcement programs to get sweatheads and purveyors of exercise equipment off the track and out of the pool and away from impressionable individuals, exercise will continue to spread like wildfire.

In a free society, laws are made by *our* representatives, and by writing, petitioning, and bribing our legislators we can get tough anti-exercise legislation on the books. One such measure, the Baskin-Robbins Bill, has been before the Senate Sedentary Committee for four years. In essence the much-needed bill calls for four sweeping reforms:

1. Cessation of trade and diplomatic relations with nations that participate in Olympic events.

1. This fact may have much to do with the increased use of tranquilizers in recent years as exercisers seek to get back "down" to an even keel.

2. The right to detain and feed individuals suspected of exercising without a warrant for their arrest.[2]

3. Mandatory death penalty for those individuals apprehended trafficking in nose-plugs, gorp, sweat suits, bee pollen, or other exercise-related paraphernalia.

4. No running, swimming, biking, skiing or rope-jumping is to be permitted in any public place.[3]

With popular support this bill will soon become law. Then, of course, exercise will become even more widespread, fashionable, and difficult to eradicate. So, we must learn.

How to stop exercising through drugs: Many of the medicines of modern science and the centuries-old remedies of herbal origin are available to duplicate and far exceed the stimulatory effects of exercise. These have the added advantage of providing experiences you can enjoy sitting down, in the aerphobic comfort of your divan, chair, toilet seat, or water bed.

Have the exerciser sample the following exercise-stimulus substitutes—all readily available substances:

1. Dexadrine
2. Coca leaves
3. Diet pills
4. Matte, coffee, and tea
5. Nutmeg and banana skins (smoked)
6. Goat-a-Gogo (texturized goat adrenal-gland extract)
7. An affair
8. A hot foot .

---

2. Evidence of sweat, saliva, or heavy breathing being sufficient to incriminate the accused.

3. Exercise would still be permissible in the privacy of one's home. However, unless you are Randolph Hearst this is rather limiting.

9. Armed assault
10. Aspirin and Coca-Cola[4]

Of course these are only temporary stop-gap measures. The true aerphobe shuns stimulants and favors depressants, relishing Maalox, naps, burgers, and relish.

4. The most dangerous stimulant combination known to man.

Aerobic Exercise and Sports

Aerobic exercise is to sports as flossing teeth is to kissing; that is, you can't have the enjoyment of the latter without undergoing the drudgery of the former. Remove the strategy, teamwork, scoring, and suspense from sport and you have aerobic exercise.

Aerobic conditioning is, of course, a factor in sports performance; basketball players must run and jump,[1] water-polo players don't fare too well if they can't swim. But our most popular participatory sports, bowling and golf, owe their success to the near-absence of exercise from them.

Exercisers persist, however, in classifying themselves as athletes, though there are a few things in life that require less skill and coordination than placing one limb in front of another. It is possible to exploit this misconception among aerobicists, thus turning their athletic interests toward more acceptable and healthy recreational activities.

Turning a swimmer, cyclist, or runner on to the thrill of bowling, for example, can be easily accomplished. The romantic ambience of the bowladrome, the festive, natty apparel from monogrammed T-shirt to felt-topped shoes, the soothing sounds of falling pins and witty between-frame repartée, conspire to lure all but the most self-punishing aerobe into tossing a few lines.

While this alternative sports therapy will prove irresist-

1. Excepting Abdul-Jabbar.

ible to most, more drastic sports therapies may occasionally be required. The Sedentary Institute of Technology reports success with such sport-aversion therapies as javelin-catching, playing second base (literally), Jell-O diving, and horseless polo.

A successful javelin-catch

It must be recognized, however, that these are but temporary substitutes, useful in breaking the aerobic exercise addiction, but in themselves aerphobically contra-indicated. All sports are exercise, even bowling, and thus potentially dangerous. Worse still, each can be obnoxiously habit forming in its own right.[2] Ultimately, the aerobic participant must be weaned from the playing field to the armchair. This can be more easily done through sports, which are more complicated and more dependent on equipment, than through minimalist aerobic exercises. A few missed court reservations at eight bucks a shot, or a broken graphite golf iron can

2. "Please pass the salt, it's on your backhand side," etc., ad nauseam.

disenchant anyone. Only a typhoon or major surgery can stop some fanatics, but these events can also be arranged. In the meantime you can begin to deal with the sportsman or woman by using these S.I.T.-endorsed substitutes for popular sporting activities:

SPORT SUBSTITUTES

ATHLETIC ACTIVITY	AERPHOBIC SUBSTITUTE
Tennis	Electronic Ping-Pong
Basketball	Tollbooth Coin Toss
Football	Foosball
Ice Hockey	Air Hockey
Water Polo	Dead Man's Float
Slalom Skiing	Chair-lift races
Golf	Miniature Golf
Baseball	Baseball Card Toss
Channel Swim	Wading
30-kilometer Road Race (on foot)	Indianapolis 500 (on TV)

Exercise and Fun

I hesitate to even mention these two antipodal concepts in the same sentence. Entertainment, or the lack thereof, is what distinguishes true sport from lowly exercise, as we've just pointed out.[1] Sport spectating, like its close relations, ogling, eyeing, leering, peering, and peeping, is a fundamental human activity. From the Circus Maximus to Barnum & Bailey, there is no posture more natural to humans than sitting down. Thanks to evolution, our forelimbs have been left free to consume popcorn, cotton candy, beer, and hot dogs.

Sports is but one aspect of entertainment. Not all athletic activity is worthy of our rapt attention. But tennis, baseball, football, even golf, regularly draw crowds on the order of the tens of thousands. Not that we are a choosy species of voyeurs; we'll even pay to watch activities that require only infinitesimal amounts of athletic skill or hominid intelligence: demolition derby, barrel-jumping, steer-wrestling, and dog-walking. All of these, for whatever bizarre psychological reasons, are of interest to members of the aerphobic masses.

But when was the last time you saw a crowd at a cross-country ski race? A bicycle rally? An English Channel swim?[2] Can't recall, can you? I thought not.

---

1. Read the sports chapter again if you forgot. You will be quizzed. And take that gum out of your mouth.
2. The large crowds at some marathons are entirely composed of relatives of the runners and emergency medical crews.

These aerobic activities are exercises, not sport, and so they do not merit watching, not to mention participating. Don't let any wild-eyed swimmer or cyclist tell you his is a sport. Apply this simple one-question test: Is it fun to watch?[3] If the answer is no, it's aerobic. If the answer is yes, it's entertainment,[4] and you'll wind up paying $12.50 for a ticket to it, sooner or later.

Still, this is a moderate price. Really expensive things are by their very nature and expense (i.e., root-canal work or testimonial dinners) *not* fun. Free things such as the Tour de France, Fukuokua Marathon, and Olympic biathlon[5] are obviously aerobic and no fun either. Makes $50.00 to see Wayne Newton at the Sahara seem like a bargain, no?

HOW TO STOP EXERCISING THROUGH FUN: In a word, sadism. Although exercise isn't fun at all, by developing sadistic appreciation, you can derive enjoyment from watching others exercise. You've got to get it through your cranium that the joy of life is *not* in the doing. There may well be no joy in life at all. If that grim sentiment proves true, the only way to have fun is to watch others suffer, and to enjoy it. Suffering is nowhere more evident than in the exercises of aerobic practitioners. And no one is in better position to watch it than the already-seated aerphobe.

Take a look around. See those grimacing, puffing, reddening faces, those cramping, sweating, hobbling bodies? Smile; it's not your problem.

---

3. As for sports in general, the question for the participant is: Is this necessary? Answer—no.
4. *That's Entertainment* is another story and costs about $3.75 in re-release.
5. A compote of sports leftovers such as cross-country skiing and shooting.

PART IV

Exercise and the Aerphobic Mind

Exercise and Psychology

What is the phrase most in the minds of observers of exercise fanatics? "You got to be out of your mind to do that!" These are words not to be taken lightly.

Many advocates believe that their exercise gives them added emotional stability, a sense of self-worth developed from discipline and what they view as improving performance and appearance. Psychologists have come to use exercise sessions as a therapeutic tool in treating many emotional disorders, including schizophrenia, acute depression, and other neuroses and psychoses.

Is exercise a tool whereby we come to know ourselves better? No.

Endurance exercise does have superficial similarities to psychoanalysis, as it must be practiced at least four times a week to be effective and leaves you pretty much where you started after expending much hot air. Though more expensive, psychoanalysis presents the clear advantage of allowing the patient to lie down.

Exercise, in fact, aggravates neurotic and psychotic tendencies in the individual psyche. Unlike television, work, or other aerphobic time-killers, exercise does not keep the mind occupied[1] and so the practitioner is left to face his gravest worries. What fears is he fleeing from? What strange fantasies is he chasing after? Who knows? Who cares?

1. A good case can be made against television, too.

Exercise is inherently anti-social and as it is most often practiced in seclusion or silence, it favors disorientation and withdrawal. The spiritual feeling claimed by some fanciers is in reality a symptom of a slackening grip on reality. The incomprehensible argot of exercisers, discussed elsewhere, may be seen as symptomatic of garbled schizophrenic speech. These people are obsessed with paranoid fears that others are gaining on them, with hypochondriacal anxieties relating to injuries, health, and weight.

In addition to fostering these disturbances, exercise can lead to several unique conditions in the disturbed patient, documented in psychiatric literature:[2]

Sedophobia. A pathological fear of relaxation, extreme form of common "ants-in-pants" syndrome.
Anorexia skinosa.[3] Potentially fatal avoidance of food, ostensibly to improve ski-race times.
Natosis. A psychotic state in which the subject is always talking about swimming, a reverse catatonia.
Peugeotphilia. An unnatural craving to be close to ten-speed bicycles.
Marancholia. Deep depression affecting competitive types who fail to qualify for Boston Marathon.

It is difficult to say which is worse: these diseases or their treatment. Fortunately, aerphobics, as always, offers an alternative.

The object of our lives, aerphobics shows us, is not heightened self-awareness, but lowered self-awareness. As the great philosopher Zuckerkandl put it, "The task is not to make people conscious of the unconscious but to make them unconscious of their conscious."[4] By habit and routine, ritual,

2. *Sweat and the Unconscious,* by Sigfried Fraud. Recorded by the Vienna Wafers on the Libidinal Label, and in paperback from ID E.O.C. Press.
3. "Skinosa" is not a pejorative Italian reference to Bob Hope.
4. *Zuckerkandl,* by Robert Maynard Hutchins. Grove Press, New York, 1969. (A real book, and a fine one.)

ignorance, and above all, sloth, we ward off any awareness of the vexing questions plaguing our inner selves, and our nasty natures. To explore the inner self through exercise is to invite deep distress. You are probably a creep—almost everybody is—so why depress yourself by finding it out?

HOW TO STOP EXERCISING THROUGH PSYCHOLOGY: Forget it.

HOW TO STOP EXERCISING THROUGH AERPHOBICS: Now that's more like it. Eat some cake, have a few belts, turn on the tube, pull out *People*, and let these aids help you blot out all consciousness. The proper program of stimulus-deprivation such as this will soon produce the sort of lasting brain damage you once could get only with a frontal lobotomy. Exertion, your worries, and conscious thought will soon be things of the past.

Exercise and Language

Just as endurance exercise leads to sexual, physiological, and psychological dysfunction, so too does it cause an impairment of mental faculties, as evidenced by a decline in language skills. Like many cults and minorities, the exercise fraternity has evolved its own slang as an immature device to assuage group insecurity and exclude the uninitiated. The similarity to the argot of drug addicts is striking; where heroin users "shoot up," the distance competitor "loads up." As can be predicted for a group so preoccupied with their physical well-being, the exerciser's slang centers on "in" terms for various physical ailments and conditions aggravated by the exercise. Particularly familiar and well documented are the ravings of runners, i.e., "I wore down my Nikes so bad I was pronating on my heel strike and I strained my quads." Less well recognized are the pat phrases of other aerobicists. "I spoke too soon," is the common complaint of cyclists who stopped racing to repair faulty wheels. "It's water under the bridge," cries the panicky swimmer whose sinuses are filling with H_2O. Many a cold-weather rope-jumper has quit for inability to get "jump-started."

On the other hand, the aerphobic mainstream's social disdain of exercise is reflected in our common idiomatic phrasing. Aerobic exercisers are encouraged to "go soak your head," "jump in the lake," "skate on thin ice," "pedal their wares elsewhere," or simply to "run for it." By no means is this idiomatic disdain of exercise limited to the English language. A simple example, which has been unfortunately twisted in English usage, is the German word "juggernaut," meaning literally "nothing-jogger" or "worthless exerciser."

The central education dilemma of our time is how we are to rid ourselves of the noisome subcultural dialect of the exercise fanatic. Fortunately, the Sedentary Institute of Technology has done much to identify and remedy—not to mention exaggerate—this problem.

HOW TO STOP EXERCISING THROUGH LANGUAGE: As a society we must assimilate the exerciser's peculiar phrases into our own speech. By appropriating the user's slang we can undermine his fragile sense of community, and so perhaps hasten the decline of the menace of exercise. In practice this can be accomplished by employing the following alternative definitions for common terms used in all aerobic sports:

A professional doing "carbohydrate-loading"

Carbohydrate-loading. Trucker's job at a Twinkie factory.

Electrolyte imbalance. All the lamps on one side of the room.

Gluteus maximus. Latin phrase meaning "big white bread."

Glycolysis. Process of mixing glycerine and rosewater to make hand lotion.

Harvard step test. Trivia quiz on the size of the entrance to Widener Library.

Heat stress. Suzanne Sommers in a bikini.

Heat stroke. Suzanne Sommers without a bikini.

Ketosis. Foul-smelling housekeys, caused by exercising with key-chain in pocket.

Krebs cycle. German motorscooter with a complicated chain.

Lactose. Front of runner or biker's foot after collision with truck.

Myoglobin. Possessive blood particles, i.e., better than youroglobin.

Orthotics. The science of lawn-care products.

Quads. Four-cornered muscles, i.e., Alan Ludden's head.

Recovery. Room where endurance exercisers frequently end up.

Exercise and Spiritual Awareness

By now we've all heard the stories of exercisers who claim mystical experiences, transcendental feelings of oneness with the universe, in the midst of a strenuous workout. They are specially attuned to all life around and within them, or so they say. This heightened awareness, the *zen* of exercise, is so nebulous and ill defined a state as to defy belief. Nevertheless, this spiritual longing, epitomized by the Exercise Transcendentalism movement (ET), is a motivational force in the recruitment of innocents which must be confronted.

As with all modern spiritual movements, ET began in Southern California in the late 1960's. Founder Guru Yamaha Ghee (formerly Ralph Sobel), claims that all great religious leaders of the world were champion endurance athletes who logged so many miles and so tuned their bodies that they were able to cross from heaven to Earth. Ghee has reinterpreted world religious literature according to these beliefs.

Ghee's religious exercise program has drawn millions of adherents worldwide, commonly known as ET-iots. Wearing sneakers and loose saffron warm-ups, they chant incessantly as they run through the streets, striving to attain a transcendental state. The refrain, so familiar to all of us, goes simply, "Hurry hurry, Hurry runner, Runner crazy, Crazy crazy."

Novice adherents to the Guru's philosophy are given a personalized prayer, or *mantis*, to repeat as they work out. Most of us have heard them saying their mantises in passing, phrases such as "Oy, vay," "Oh! My heart!" and "A half-mile more" being common examples.

Most member's of Ghee's ET movement have joined through one of the weekly introductory seminars, at a cost of $2,500. Proceeds from the course, ET-sponsored God Races, and the ET monthly magazine *Vishnews* are disbursed by Guru Ghee from his Bel Air home. The Guru himself does not exercise, having reached a level of transcendence where the mere thought of running renders him weak with spiritual insight. Ghee is a highly visible leader, as he weighs 435 pounds, drives a pink Rolls-Royce, and is a frequent guest on the Johnny Carson Show.

The appeal of Exercise Transcendentalism, whether as a part of Ghee's group, or some more personal grail, is based upon a fundamental misconception about the role of religion in our lives. Aerphobics teaches us an opposing theological concept.

The aerphobe does not seek to find God in his life. Rather he takes it easy and leaves plenty of room and work for Him, if He cares to visit. To the aerphobicist, God is not a debatable, or uncertain force from whom we seek manifestations, miracles, and guidance.

God's presence, to the aerphobe, has already been amply demonstrated. If He didn't exist, how do we know His name, and use it in vain? God was definitely here. He left us several good books, a few miracles, some decent movie adaptations, a host of aliases, and in His image, Charlton Heston.

He's not dead to aerphobicists, He's just exhausted. "Give the Guy a break," is *the* religious tenet of the aerphobic population.

Perhaps if we bothered Him less, say the aerphobes, He might return. Now He's just saving on the long-distance calls, speaking only occasionally to Anita Bryant, and His alter ego, Danny Thomas.

And why worry about His return? If He's going to come back, He'll have the decency to phone ahead, if only to make reservations and get tickets for *Annie*. So aerphobicists go comfortably about their ways, content in the knowledge that should God ever choose to enter our lives, He'd knock first and leave us plenty of time to clean up our acts.

HOW TO STOP EXERCISING THROUGH RELIGION: If you are starved for spiritual insight, try substituting other less habit-forming rituals of observance for exercise. Give your salary to Herbert Muhammed, listen to "Sermonette," observe Yom Kippur several times a week, or simply honk. If these accepted religious practices don't frustrate or bore you out of all spiritual longings, an alternative strategy is recommended.

Enroll in a modern French existential literature class at the nearest university. A careful explication and selected readings of Sartre, Camus, and Beckett will fill you with such a sense of international ennui and angst that you will soon disavow all religious beliefs. *Warning:* Be careful to enroll in only a semester's course, as a full year often ends in suicide.

PART V

Exercise in an Aerphobic World

Exercise and Success

The formula for success is composed of varying amounts of money, fame, and love,[1] usually in that order. Exercise is at best irrelevant and more often counterproductive to each of these elements of achievement. We have dealt elsewhere with the sorry love lives of aerobicists so let us give celebrity and wealth the once-over.

Making money is often spoken of as an obsession in modern America. Obsessions are full-time jobs, and if you are lucky enough to have one, you don't need a distraction such as an exercise habit. There is simply no way money can be made by working out. Next time you have the boss over for dinner ask him if he exercises. Chances are the answer will be an emphatic "no!" Making others, like you, sweat, is what got him where he is.

As for full-time devotion to aerobic exercises, they encompass only those lowly sports[2] which present no hope of remuneration. Compare the approximated annual salaries of these athletes:

Jimmy Connors (tennis)	$750,000
O. J. Simpson (football)	650,000
Reggie Jackson (baseball)	600,000
Kareem Abdul-Jabbar (basketball)	600,000

1. See the game *Careers* for more precise equation figures.
2. Nonaerobic nonremunerative games include tiddlywinks, newcombe, dodgeball, and *Careers*.

Xaviera Hollander[3] (acrobatics)	550,000
Jack Nicklaus (golf)	350,000
Richard Petty (auto racing)	250,000
Earl Anthony (bowling)	100,000
Gabriel Kaplan[4] (embarrassing)	55,000
Frank Shorter (running)	expenses
Kornelia Ender (swimming)	0

There is no financial reward for being a top practitioner of aerobic exercise, but the vast majority of adherents are not even competitive at it. They limit their competitive participation to an occasional race, in which they actually *pay* for the privilege of exhausting themselves. In logical terms this is the equivalent of shelling out forty bucks for a Super Bowl ticket and then having Mean Joe Greene toss you out of your seat.

Nor is endurance training anything but a marathon route to fame. Look around at your companions next time you work out. Are these the beautiful people? Heaven help us if they are.

Lasting notoriety accrues to those who perform acts of originality or deviance, and who are themselves commanding, memorable presences. These requirements are far better filled by aerphobes than by runners, skiers, swimmers, or bicyclists. Can you name a single great public figure who is accomplished at one of these endurance sports?[5] Neither can I, as the following list indicates:

FAMOUS AEROBICISTS[6]	FAMOUS AERPHOBES
	Nero
	Henry VIII
	Boss Tweed
	William Howard Taft
	Hermann Goering

3. Not counting tips.
4. From Superstars competition only.
5. Jimmy Carter the jogger and Jerry Ford the swimmer don't qualify on either end.
6. Slim Pickens indeed.

FAMOUS AEROBICISTS	FAMOUS AERPHOBES
	Nikita Khrushchev
	Mao Tse-Tung
	Peter Ustinov
	Orson Welles
	Alfred Hitchcock
	Sydney Greenstreet
	Kate Smith
	"Fats" Domino
	Minnesota "Fats"
	"Fats" Waller
	"Fatty" Arbuckle

HOW TO STOP EXERCISING THROUGH SUCCESS: First get successful. How you do it is your business; there are plenty of books out on that subject also. Now that you are, *do not* hire a social secretary. People will be calling you all day, wanting you to: come to their parties so they can be seen with you, sit in while Johnny's on vacation, or more often asking you to join them for lunch so they can get a job, autograph, favor, date, or lunch. Without a social secretary to put these people off, you will find yourself so busy with meetings that you won't have time to exercise.

Exercise and Economics

I'll be blunt: aerobic exercise is un-American. For the benefit of those who have been working out in ignorance of its political significance, I will briefly explain.

The American way of life (God's way also) is the capitalist free-enterprise system. Our economic well-being depends upon the full participation of the individual consumer. As individuals, we seek to work ever-shorter hours to provide us with money to support and entertain ourselves in aerphobic style during our leisure time.[1]

During this leisure time we spend all our money and then some on products evolved through American ingenuity: Twinkies, Budweiser, snowmobiles, and Yamahas to name a few.

The aerobicist sees him or herself as apart from the mainstream of American leisure life. Aerobic exercise requires no equipment, save for a pair of shoes, a bicycle, skis, or swimsuit, and those are often imported. The patriotic, public-spirited downhill ski nut spends more on lift tickets in a day than a cross-countryist forks over annually. Skiers' dollars lead to jobs from lift–ticket-taker to construction such as the nearby McDonald's chalets, and to inventions, such as the snow-making machines which extend the ski season. The skier drives to the slope, rides the chair lift, sleeps in a Holiday Inn, and checks into the area hospital to have his

1. Also known as lazy-faire economics.

126

fracture set. All those activities are recreation-related income, helping to keep our economy strong.

Exercisers often acquire abstemious habits which further undermine our system. They eat less and avoid the high-cost packaged and prepared foods for fear that they are unhealthy. Exercisers often report an increased sense of overall self-sufficiency and independence. This, of course, is a delusion and is dealt with elsewhere in the book. From an economic standpoint, this attitude means less money for psychiatry, TM, and other support and counseling institutions such as bars and pharmacies. The aerobics-related decline in alternative therapies alone might sink the economy of California.

Researchers from the Sedentary Institute of Technology have computer-tabulated a Consumer-Related Activity Prediction forecasting the disappearance of many staples of American life should the exercise phenomenon continue to spread. Ten key indicators to watch for declining incidence are:

1. Size 18's
2. Whipped cream
3. Escalators
4. Between-meal treats
5. Disco-trimmers
6. Bowladromes
7. Pacemakers
8. Electric carving-knives
9. Dunkin' Donuts
10. Naps

Aerobic exercise is anti-social, anti-consumer, and therefore anti-American. Your country asks that you not work out. Will you obey? If not, a suggestion:

How to stop exercising through politics: There is only one American way to work out and that is to run for office. This is a short spurt followed by years of less strenuous exercises such as arm-twisting, pigeon-holing, stonewalling, back-scratching, and, back-stabbing. Successful office-runners occasionally also practice the kick-back stroke, but do so exclusively from the pork barrel in smoke-filled rooms, an enviably aerphobic life-style. Once safely ensconced in American political life via these exercises, the one-time runner becomes a "fat cat" and need put only minimal effort into a single run every two, four, or six years.

Exercise and Literature

Literature, said F. R. Leavis, is the first distinction of a civilized man. The written word is often cited as man's most distinguishing accomplishment; exercise never is. We have always striven to find a single distinctive feature separating us from the rest of nature. Many of these distinctions we now know to be false. We are not the only tool-users, the only speakers, the only upright walkers, or painters. We are, however, the only species capable of writing *War and Peace,* even though we may lack the patience to read it. It is all but impossible to name a best seller written by another animal.[1]

Physical exertion and physical play in childhood are common denominators of the animal kingdom,[2] part of an instinctual "flight or fight" mechanism. Exercisers, we note, have chosen to retain only the cowardly half of this drive.

Unlike exercise, literature preserves and spreads individual ideas and feelings and so shapes our collective lives. We find inspiration and guidance in our daily lives from literary classics such as *The Bible, How to Be Your Own Best Friend,* and Sidney Omarr's *Daily Horoscope.* In works such as these we can find specific recommendations from those wiser and more experienced than us on every facet of life, including even exercise. To ignore this sage advice is to risk paying the price of hubris,[3] so read on; be forewarned.

1. Harold Robbins notwithstanding.
2. Even amoebas have feet (pseudopods).
3. $99.95, inquire at Birnham Woods Country Club.

HOW TO STOP EXERCISING THROUGH LITERATURE: Commit these passages to memory. What exerciser could contradict the word of Shakespeare, the great poets, or the Lord?[4] The Devil may be able to quote Scriptures to suit his own purposes, but the average semi-literate aerobicist cannot. "But I, I cannot read . . . although I run and run," ("Song of the Strange Ascetic," by G. K. Chesterton). You have no reason to fear contradiction:

Aerphobic Quote Book

The Scriptures warn us of the coming of an exercise fad:[5]
"Gentiles exercise"—Luke 22:25.[6]

Still, says the author, "I do not exercise myself . . ." —Book of Common Prayer, Psalm 130.

Apparently, the Dead Sea Float was not in vogue, and ski conditions were not optimal on Mt. Ararat, for running appears to be the predominant exercise of the time.[7] The deviant and dangerous types drawn to running are described:

(Thieves) "Their feet run to evil"—Isaiah 59:7.

(Murderers) "Angry fellows run upon thee, and thou lose thy life"—Judges 18:25.

(Madmen) "They shall run upon the wall"—Joel 2:9.

By Shakespearean times, running had attracted a renewed cast of cowards, fools, madmen, and thieves:

"Now like to whelps, we crying run . . ."—*Henry I*, William Shakespeare.

"I have instructed cowards to run"—*Anthony and Cleopatra, Ibid.*[8]

"The knave turns fool that runs."—*King Lear, Ibid.*

---

4. Or whoever wrote all the Good Books.
5. And according to some, just about everything else.
6. Jews apparently knew better.
7. You can't swim when the waters are parted.
8. You remember Ibid and Idem, a couple of unoriginal guys.

"Let the thief run mad"—"Rape of Lucrece," *Ibid*.

"As they run they look behind . . . they hear a voice in every wind"—"Ode on a Distant Prospect of Eton College," Thomas Gray.

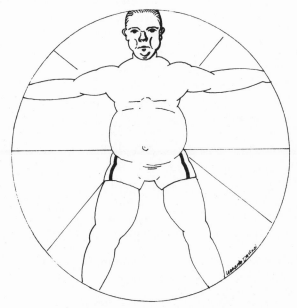

Fitting of Self to Sphere by Leonardo da Vinci:
study for *Last Brunch* mural

While skiing was evidently too small potatoes to attract the attention of epigrammists, the masters also had some choice words for other aerobic specialties: swimming, cycling, and rope-skipping. For biking, one quote suffices:

"Better 50 years of Europe than a cycle"—"Locksley Hall," Alfred Lord Tennyson.

As for swimming:

"A solitary shriek, a bubbling cry of some strong swimmer in his agony"—"Don Juan," Lord Byron.

"The arena swims around him and he is gone"—"Childe Harold," *Ibid*.

"Good swimmers are oftenest drowned"— *Dictionary Gnomologia* (c. 1729), Thomas Fuller.

"Good swimmers at the length feed Haddocks"—Randle Cotsgrave (c. 1611).

And a word of advice for young paddlers:

"Mother, may I go out to swim?"
"Yes, my darling daughter;
Hang your clothes on a hickory limb,
But don't go near the water." —Anon.

Jumping rope doesn't rate much higher:

"I will not jump with the . . . barbarous multitude."— *Merchant of Venice*, William Shakespeare.

If you must jump, don't do it at opportunities or bargains, but do as the young man who said:

"It is my fixed intent to jump as Mr. Levi did from off the Monument." —Anon.

The aerphobic life-style, on the other hand, though not yet scientifically outlined, was inherently appealing to the sagacious bards:

"Anything for a quiet life"—Thomas Middleton.

"We shall rest . . . Lie down for an eon or two"—"When Earth's Last Picture," Rudyard Kipling.

"Who doth not crave for rest"—"Paradise," Frederick William Faber.

"While I sit lazy by"—*The Tempest*, William Shakespeare.

"Everyone to rest themselves . . . save thieves"—"Rape of Lucrece," William Shakespeare.

The interplay of inertia and the development of the ideal aerphobic physique was eloquently summed up thus:

"Rest is the fitting of self to its sphere"—"True Rest," John S. Dwight.

But let's give the last word to the Word:

"Wash your feet and rest."—Genesis 18:4.

Exercise and Prejudice

Though this book was designed with American audiences in mind, exercise is a worldwide health problem of long standing. The pantheon of noted addicts—Scandinavian cross-country skiers, Kenyan distance runners, East German women swimmers, and Italian bicyclists, to name but a few nationalities[1]—reflects the international nature of the disease.

Far be it from this book to deal in ethnic stereotyping, but exercisers of various ethnic backgrounds should be aware of the insulting thoughts, spoken and unspoken, which they are engendering in the minds of millions of narrow-minded spectators. We present these distasteful comments in the hope that they will persuade runners to desist from pursuing actions which only serve to inflame regional, national, and racial prejudices:

EXERCISER'S ANCESTRY — SPECTATOR'S REMARKS

Mexican. "I knew they sleepwalk, but this . . ."
Swiss. "I thought they had Turks do their exercise for them."
Chinese. "No room to move over there, huh?"
English. "I don't know how they do it with a poker up . . ."
Protestant. "Harder, you're not working."
Catholic. "Lousy rhythm!"
Jewish. "Slow down, it's only a slug."

1. Four to be precise.

New Yorker. "Faster, they're gaining!"
New Englander. "You can't get there from here."
Southerner. "Pull over, boy."
Californian. "Stop. You're passé."
Northwesterner. "Quick, before it rains."
Eskimo. "Got to run off that blubber, huh?"
Indian. "On the warpath, chief?"
Polish. Unprintable.

HOW TO QUIT EXERCISING THROUGH PREJUDICE: Knowing that people are thinking such vile thoughts about you or your friends should be sufficiently sickening to sour you on working out. If you have not been exposed to such prejudice because you are part of a highly homogeneous community, you may wish to inspire such exercise-alienating prejudice by disguising yourself as a conspicuous minority-member and exercising. Most-hated status varies considerably by region, but for those who desire one particular get-up for a variety of environments, a Jewish outfit is the best bet.[2]

Alternatively, you may simply think back to the last time you worked out. Remember that guy who sped by? There was something different about him, wasn't there? Maybe he was trying to show you up? Aren't all of *them* trying to show us up? They're probably waiting, right now, for you to start going, so they can outdo you. Are you going to give them that satisfaction? Hell, no! No more exercise for you. Let them sweat themselves silly; you quit.

---

2. Hence the name "Chosen People." For further information see (or better, hear) Tom Lehrer's "National Brotherhood Week" from the album *That Was the Year That Was*.

Exercise and Etiquette

Rules of etiquette have evolved in modern society to govern proper behavior in all forms of social interaction, from how to address the Pope[1] if he should show up unexpectedly for dinner, to what to do with things that fall out of your nose while you are talking to someone.

But because aerobics is such a recent popular phenomenon, and since Emily Post is dead, there were, until this writing, few accepted rules of behavior for such exercises. Here, at last, are ten:

1. Always keep your pinkie elevated while moving.

2. When addressing a female participant refer to her as Madam Jogger (Swimmer, etc.), or by nonsexist titles such as Fellow Exerciser, or in Eastern Europe, Comrade Plodder. Do not use the terms "babe," "toots," or "slow-poke."

3. Address a male exerciser of noble lineage as Your Spryness, otherwise Mister Exerciser will do. "Bub," "chief," "captain," and "meatball" are unacceptable.

4. All gentlemen exercisers should wear an ascot or loose-fitting cravat, spats, and cap.

5. Female participants are advised to wear floor-length dress, and tight, concealing undergarments, including corset.

6. Before passing another, cough and whisper quietly, "May I overtake you?" Pass on left, sound horn.

7. When approaching an exerciser from the opposite

1. No hints, but it isn't "Hiya, Pops."

direction, it is proper to pass on the right, but not before stopping, bowing, and inquiring as to the other's health.

8. A gentleman, in the company of a lady, exercises on her right.

9. Never expectorate while exercising. If it's unavoidable, do so discreetly into a white hankie. Never "gob" onto another's feet.

10. Stop for children and older exercisers passing in either direction. Assist them by pummeling all pets and wildlife in vicinity.

How to stop exercising through etiquette: If you really believe in etiquette, you'll never finish saying your good-byes to guests in time to go work out. You certainly won't want to work up a sweat.

But etiquette, as any aerphobe worth his brew will tell you, is a bunch of crap. In aerphobics there is no such thing as etiquette. You belch when you want to, which is pretty nearly always. You don't get out of your chair when someone comes in the room; you couldn't even if you tried. You don't worry about which is the salad fork, since you don't eat salad, and you don't use silverware. If you want somebody or something you don't bother with titles; the only titled person you talk about is Duke Snider. Others you refer to as they do you, by affectionate names of non-sexist, nonparticular use, such as "Fats," "Tiny," and "Porkie."[2]

The informality of the aerphobic life-style is but one of its many attractions. Leave etiquette to the exercisers; get fat, and get rude.

2. Or you can just grunt.

PART VI

Toward an Aerphobic Future
(An End to Exercisers)

Desperate Measures

If the addiction of your mate is the one in a million that does not respond to any of the quit-exercise treatments outlined previously in this book, you may wish to try the following phrases on the addict before he or she sets out:

The milkman cometh while hubby exercises

1. "Wait, I'll go with you."

2. "I put your equipment in the wash." (A lame excuse unless you really do it.)

3. "Does your knee *feel* swollen?"

4. "What does 'air quality hazardous' mean?"

Or:

WIFE: 5a. "The plumber was here." (Tear nightgown slightly.)

HUSBAND: 5b. "I was over at Madge's to borrow sugar." (Smear lipstick on cheek, or if double-jointed give yourself a hickey.)

More Desperate Measures

If the lines on the preceding page didn't do the trick, you may wish to try these sure-fire solutions to the exercise problem:

1. Squash the addict's toes with a ball peen hammer.
2. Have the addict commit a felony. (There's no room to run in maximum security.)
3. Lash the addict to the wheel of the car.
4. Lock the addict in a Viennese bakery for a month.
5. Move to Venice.

Motion denied

The Final Solution

When all else fails, there remains but one certain cure for the addicted exerciser—death. When all other therapies outlined here have failed, those who live with the exercise addict truly have no alternative but to put him or her out of his or her misery, and end the suffering he or she inflicts upon family, friends, and the community. Any judge with an ounce of compassion would rule such a mercy killing to be justifiable homicide, but it's possible to avoid messy legal entanglements by having the exerciser induce his or her own demise.

HOW TO STOP EXERCISING THROUGH DEATH: All you need do is persuade the exerciser to try the new experience of Blindfolded Exercise. Affix the blindfold firmly over the eyes, and let 'em go.

Causes and frequencies of deaths resulting from blindfolded workouts vary according to the exercise and the particular topographic conditions. Swimmers may need to have their hands tied to allow for maximum surprise turn-impact, and urban cyclists and runners will most often meet the Grim Reaper where drivers are least skilled in avoiding them (i.e., Boston), or most intent on hitting them (i.e., Montgomery).

Most drivers are slow to grasp the suicidal intentions of the blindfolded exerciser and will take all steps, short of delaying their trip, to avoid the unfortunate. You may wish to provoke them by having the exerciser wear nothing, or suitable slogans, such as "Hit me, I'm Irish," and binding appendages into obscene gestural positions.

In rural areas where traffic is not a major hazard, cross-country blindfold cycling is recommended. Cycling to death can be especially difficult in some rural areas, such as the Midwest, where the enthusiast may go for days without encountering an obstacle more imposing than an amber wave of grain. However, the runner may be effectively snuffed out in such locales by threshing combines, stud bulls, electric fencing, or sheer boredom.

In many rural areas, trees are the most effective deterrent in canceling the blinded cyclist's check. Hardwoods such as oak and apple are best, the soft pines being virtually useless.

Blindfold cyclist experiences "hitting the wall"

Coastal blindfold cyclists are at an obvious advantage provided they are first oriented toward the water.[1]

For the fortunate who can afford the trip, the rain-forest mountain-lake country of Guatemala is perhaps the best suited terrain on Earth for running to self-destruction, being a fortuitous blend of disease, danger, isolation, and impassable topography.

If you have remembered to properly insure[2] your fallen mate, you are now on your way to a contented, exercise-free, aerphobic future. *Bon appétit!*

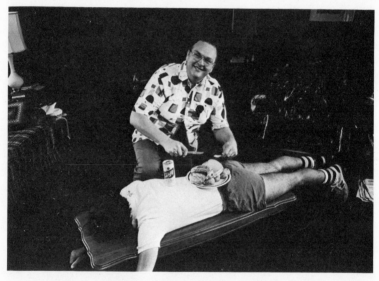

To the victor belongs the snack

1. See *The Fatal Impact*, by Alan Morebooks.
2. S.I.T. offers a budget life-insurance plan. For information call Linkletter Low-Life, at the toll-free number 800-555-0000. Ask for Vito.